Confronting Equality

Confronting Equality

Gender, Knowledge and Global Change

RAEWYN CONNELL

polity

First published in 2011 by Polity Press

Polity Press
65 Bridge Street
Cambridge CB2 1UR, UK

Polity Press
350 Main Street
Malden, MA 02148, USA

ISBN-13: 978-0-7456-5350-1 (hardback)
ISBN-13: 978-0-7456-5351-8 (paperback)

A catalogue record for this book is available from the British Library.

Typeset in 11 on 13 pt Monotype Bembo
by Servis Filmsetting Ltd, Stockport, Cheshire
Printed and bound in Great Britain by MPG Books Group Limited, Bodmin, Cornwall

The publisher has used its best endeavours to ensure that the URLs for external websites referred to in this book are correct and active at the time of going to press. However, the publisher has no responsibility for the websites and can make no guarantee that a site will remain live or that the content is or will remain appropriate.

Every effort has been made to trace all copyright holders, but if any have been inadvertently overlooked the publisher will be pleased to include any necessary credits in any subsequent reprint or edition.

For further information on Polity, visit our website: www.politybooks.com

Contents

Introduction   *page* 1

1 Change among the Gatekeepers: Men, Masculinities
   and Gender Equality   7
2 Steering towards Equality? How Gender Regimes
   Change inside the State   25
3 The Neoliberal Parent: Mothers and Fathers in Market
   Society   41
4 Working-Class Families and the New Secondary
   Education   58
5 Good Teachers on Dangerous Ground   73
6 Not the Pyramids: Intellectual Workers Today   89
7 Sociology has a World History   103
8 Paulin Hountondji's Postcolonial Sociology of
   Knowledge   119
9 Antonio Negri's Theory of Empire   136
10 Bread and Waratahs: A Letter to the Next Left   154

Acknowledgements   167
References   170
Index   187

Introduction

Late in 2009, the United Nations convened a great meeting in Copenhagen on an issue being defined as the greatest challenge of our time. Specialists in climate science had warned for years about the growing turbulence and risk resulting from human activities that change and especially heat the atmosphere. After two weeks of bitter wrangling, the governments of the world went home, having agreed on almost nothing. Developing countries, led by China, refused more restrictions on their high-pollution drive for economic growth; rich countries, led by the United States, refused the demand to wind down their high-consumption way of life.

In mid 2010, the British-based transnational oil corporation BP had a nasty accident at an underwater well in the Gulf of Mexico, resulting from the urgent search for more fossil fuel as the time of 'peak oil' approaches. A media blitz followed the threat of pollution to the southern coast of the United States. A few media stories – only a few – drew a parallel with the catastrophe that had already surrounded oil spills on another continent. The Niger River delta has been the scene of epic corruption, social dislocation, civil war and devastating pollution since the oil companies arrived in the 1950s.

These traumatic events are not bad luck and not failures of personal leadership. They are consequences of the way our institutions and structures work: decisions in the hands of small elites, global struggle for profits and power, massive inequalities of resources, and the triumph of short-term calculation. We do not have a global environment problem, really. We have a global *social* problem. Ecological crisis and injustice can only be solved by social action and institutional change.

The spread of HIV/AIDS, to take another critical issue, is not just a medical problem. From the early years of the epidemic it was clear that only social action could stop it. Community mobilizations did stop it, in some places – but not widely enough. The global epidemic continues to spread through social pathways formed by poverty, violence and patriarchy.

Across a broad range of other issues, people grappling with practical dilemmas need to understand large-scale social processes. Women in organizations facing the 'glass ceiling', teachers troubled about over-surveillance of their work, activists dealing with domestic violence, knowledge workers grappling with marginality, all are stronger if they have reliable knowledge about how the problems arose and why they are intractable.

That argument motivates the research discussed in this book. We need social science because social processes shape human destinies. If we are to take control of our future, we need to understand society as much as we need to understand the atmosphere, the earth, and men's and women's bodies.

There are many dubious interpretations of the social world on offer. There is market ideology, where every problem has the same solution – private property and unrestrained markets. There is 'virtual sociology' (skewered by Judith Stacey in her recent book *Unhitched*) where pressure-groups select the research results they like, ignore the ones they don't, and so present their own prejudices as scientific findings. The most enjoyable pseudoscience is the pop sociology of market research firms: Generation X, Generation Y, the creative class, the mommy track, the metrosexuals, the sensitive new-age guy, the new traditionals, the aspirationals, the sea-changers . . . The names usually define faintly recognizable types, or at any rate marketing strategies, and the audience in wealthy countries fill in the details for themselves.

Social science is harder. It is slower. Knowledge grows by a collective process of exploration that is complex and uncertain. Research *must* be unpredictable, since we never know at the start what the results will be. (If we do know, it isn't research!) Social science needs patience and it does not suit media deadlines. It also needs resources, especially people and time. For intellectual work to be done there has to be a workforce; and that is not easily assembled or kept in being. There is often an awkward gap between significant questions and the means of answering them.

Research is usually imagined as the gathering of data, but there is much more to it. Clarifying language, generating new concepts, relating ideas to each other, building interpretations – these too are necessary steps in producing knowledge. Theory is often handed over, with a sigh of relief, to a small group of specialists. It shouldn't be. Theory is basically about trying to think beyond the immediately given; and this is business that concerns everyone with a stake in social science. In my experience, the best theoretical ideas bubble up in the midst of empirical research or practical problems and start talking to the facts straight away.

The theories most widely used in social science come from Europe and North America. This is increasingly recognized as a problem. We have become conscious of the imperial history of social science itself and the limitations of vision in even the greatest thinkers of the global North. There is now a vigorous and exciting debate about how to create a world social science that mobilizes the social experience and intellectual resources of the South – where, after all, most of the people live.

This book moves across the spectrum from empirical research to the global politics of knowledge. Three chapters report field studies: on gender equity in the public sector, school education and intellectual labour. Two chapters report documentary studies: on changing ideas about good teachers, and the global history of sociology. Two chapters try to synthesize a research field: on men's involvement with gender equality, and parent–child relations under neoliberalism. Two chapters examine remarkable contemporary thinkers: Paulin Hountondji and Antonio Negri.

The book is an attempt to show social science at work – perhaps I should say, a social scientist at work, since it is a cross-section of my recent working life. While each chapter stands in its own right (most are based on articles in professional journals), as a collection they raise personal and political questions. I have therefore ended with an explicitly political essay, a meditation on the Australian left, that grows out of my own involvement.

The diversity of these chapters is deliberate. I hope to show how a realist approach can work across different issues and in different types of investigation. So I should say a few words about the approach to social science that links them.

Social practices – including labour, care and struggle – are endlessly bringing new realities into existence. This is easily said, difficult to keep in mind. It is easier to think of the world as composed of things that we bump against like rocks – a family, a bank, a population, capitalism, patriarchy.

But the storm of time keeps blowing: not only destroying what previously appeared solid, but creating and destroying and creating again. Borrowing a slightly pompous word from the Czech philosopher Karel Kosík (1976), I call this the ontoformativity of social practice. Our collective actions, shaped by social structures precipitated from the past, *make* the social world we are moving into. And this social world is not a performative illusion, it becomes new fact. Social practice is generative, fecund, rich in real consequences.

This is frightening, as many of the consequences are dire. The last hundred years have generated the most intense moments of violence (Kursk, Hiroshima) and the worst famines in human history, as well as the deepening disaster of climate change. Yet the same century has seen the greatest-ever increase in literacy and the greatest increase in expectations of life. Huge empires have been dismantled; there has been an unprecedented global struggle towards gender equality; there is tremendous cultural inventiveness, even in very poor and disrupted communities (for magnificent proof, Vivien Johnson, *Lives of the Papunya Tula Artists*, 2008).

Social science, concerned with this reality, has to be empirical;

it tries to discover and describe the way things are in the world. The accuracy of its statements matters, its claims have to be testable and, ultimately, tested. That is what distinguishes social science from ideologies and pseudo-sciences, however entertaining or persuasive those may be.

It is usually quantitative researchers who emphasize the empirical character of social science. I value the distributive information that surveys and censuses give, and some will be found in this book. A democratic science must be concerned with all the people, not just an iconic few. But social science cannot be only a system of quantitative statements. That would mean a sadly thin form of knowledge, missing out everything that *produces* the distributions our statistical methods describe – missing, in fact, the ontoformativity of practice.

We need empirical methods that allow the creative surge through time to emerge. I have particularly used life-history interviews (chapters 2, 4 and 6), combined with organizational ethnography, survey research and policy analysis in different studies. There are other ways to do it, of course.

In this approach, the purpose of research is to illuminate *situations*, i.e. moments within the historical process that we call social reality. What social science produces, when working at full stretch, might be called *social diagnoses* – accounts of the dynamics of well-understood situations.

This approach is relevant to studying theory itself. In the conceptual chapters towards the end of the book, I look at social theories as creative responses to historical situations, whether by individual theorists or intellectual movements. This is the core of the argument against the Northern monopoly in theory – a monopoly that instals a privileged set of diagnoses as paradigms for the whole world.

This would hardly matter, if social science were just a remote contemplation of human affairs. I don't think we can afford this. Good social science, to me, means social science engaged with the world it studies.

There are researchers who believe that to be scientific one must be neutral, because politics means bias. Science does need objectivity, but objectivity does not come from neutrality. Here I follow Max Deutscher's (1983: 2) sharp criticism of the belief that objectivity means detachment. Objectivity, as the attitude that leads to accurate, adequate knowledge of people and things, actually *requires engagement* with people and things.

'Democracy' is a word so contaminated by apologists for the rich and powerful that I hesitate to use it. But the principle remains and there is no better name – a world ruled by all the people who live in it, not by a privileged minority.

No one who remembers the racism of colonialist anthropology or sociology's surveillance of the poor, or who looks at economics now, would assume social science necessarily works for democracy. But social science *can*. Research can map the dynamics of the HIV epidemic for communities struggling to control it. Research can document power structures and the machinery of privilege. Social science has some capacity to multiply the voices heard in public arenas. And social theory has a capacity to bring imagination into dialogue with current reality. Doing social theory always means recognizing that things could be otherwise; that – to borrow a phrase again – another world is possible.

For some years sociologists have been debating Michael Burawoy's (2005) idea of 'public sociology'. In that debate, public sociology figures as a choice for the social scientists (Clawson *et al.* 2007). I would put the emphasis the other way around: social science is a necessity for the public. In a world where massive social institutions and social structures shape the fate of huge populations, a participatory democracy needs powerful and accurate knowledge about society. Only with this knowledge can collective decisions be made that steer our societies on the dangerous ground of the future.

I am not suggesting that social science can be a political movement. It is a type of intellectual work, nothing more. But nothing less. It is work which produces a kind of knowledge that has become vital. Clarity and depth of understanding on social issues matter more than ever. I hope some will be found in this book.

Raewyn Connell
Sydney, August 2010

1

Change among the Gatekeepers: Men, Masculinities and Gender Equality

Equality between women and men has been an international legal principle since the 1948 Universal Declaration of Human Rights, and enjoys popular support in many countries. The idea that *men* might have a specific role in relation to this principle has only emerged recently.

Gender equality was placed on the policy agenda by women. The reason is obvious: it is women who are disadvantaged by the main patterns of gender inequality and who therefore have the claim for redress. But men are necessarily involved. Moving towards a gender-equal society involves profound institutional change as well as change in everyday life and personal conduct, and therefore requires widespread social support.

Further, the very gender inequalities in economic assets, political power, cultural authority and the means of coercion that gender reforms intend to change currently mean that men (often, specific groups of men) control most of the resources required to implement women's claims for justice. Men and boys are in significant ways gatekeepers for gender equality. Whether they are willing to open the gates for major reforms is a strategic question.

This chapter traces the emergence of a worldwide discussion of men and gender-equality reform and assesses the prospects of reform strategies involving men. To do this, we need to examine how men and boys have been understood, the politics of 'men's movements', the divided interests of men and boys in gender relations, and the research evidence about the changing and conflict-ridden social construction of masculinities.

This chapter grows out of practical policymaking, as well as research. In 2003–4 I was involved in United Nations discussions of 'the role of men and boys in achieving gender equality'. This culminated in a 2004 meeting that produced the first world-level policy document on this question. I will discuss the details later.

Men and masculinities in the world gender order

In the 1990s, in the global metropole, there was a wave of popular concern about men and boys. The US poet Robert Bly published a book *Iron John: A Book about Men* (1990), which became a huge best-seller and set off a wave of imitations. Bly's book was popular because it offered, in prophetic language, simple solutions to problems that were increasingly troubling the culture.

Specific issues about men and boys also attracted public attention in the rich countries. Men's responses to feminism, and to gender equality policies, have been debated in Germany and Scandinavia (Metz-Göckel and Müller 1985; Holter 2003). In English-speaking countries there has been enthusiasm for 'the new fatherhood' and doubt about real changes in men's involvement in families (McMahon 1999). There has been public agonizing about boys' supposed 'failure' in school, and many proposals for special programs for boys (Frank and Davison 2007). Men's violence towards women has been the subject of practical interventions and extensive debate (Hearn 1998) and men's relationship with the law is in question (Collier 2010). There has also been increasing debate about men's health and illness from a gender perspective (Hurrelmann and Kolip 2002).

Accompanying these debates has been a remarkable growth of research about men's gender identities and practices, masculinities and the social processes by which they are constructed. Academic journals have been founded for specialized research, there have been many conferences and there is a growing international literature. We now have a far more sophisticated and detailed scientific understanding of issues about men, masculinities and gender than before (Connell 2005a).

This set of concerns is found worldwide. Debates on violence, patriarchy and ways of changing men's conduct have occurred in countries as diverse as India, Germany, Canada and South Africa. Issues about masculine sexuality and fatherhood have been debated and researched across Latin America. A men's centre with a reform agenda was established in Japan, where conferences have been held and media debates about traditional patterns of masculinity and family life continue (Menzu Senta 1997). A 'travelling seminar' discussing issues about men, masculinities and gender equality toured India (Roy 2003).

The research effort is also worldwide. Differing constructions of masculinity have been documented by researchers on every continent, literally. The first global synthesis, in the form of a world handbook of research on men and masculinities, was published in 2005 (Kimmel, Hearn and Connell 2005). The work continues, for instance in recent research on the representation of men and masculinity in Indonesian culture (Clark 2010).

The rapid internationalization of these debates reflects the fact – increasingly recognized in feminist thought – that gender relations themselves have an international dimension. Change in gender relations occurs on a world scale, though not always in the same direction or at the same pace.

The dynamics of the world gender order affect men as profoundly as women, though this fact has been less discussed. Studies such as Matthew Gutmann's (2002) ethnographic work in poor communities in Mexico, show in fine detail how the lives of particular groups of men are shaped by globally acting economic and political forces.

Different groups of men are positioned very differently in these dynamics. There is no single formula that accounts for 'men and globalization'. There is, indeed, a growing polarization among men on a world scale. Studies of ruling-class men (Donaldson and Poynting 2007) show a privileged minority with astonishing wealth and power, while much larger numbers face poverty, cultural dislocation, disruption of family relationships and forced renegotiation of the meanings of masculinity.

Masculinities are socially constructed patterns of gender practice. These patterns are created through a historical process with a global dimension. The old-style 'ethnographic' research that located gender patterns purely in a local context is inadequate to the reality. Historical research, such as Robert Morrell's (2001b) study of the masculinities of the colonizers in South Africa and T. Dunbar Moodie's (1994) study of the colonized, shows how a gendered culture is created and transformed in relation to the international economy and the political system of empire. There is every reason to think this principle holds for contemporary masculinities.

Shifting ground: men and boys in gender equality debates

In both national and international policy documents concerned with gender equality, women are the subjects of the policy discourse. The agencies or meetings that formulate, implement or monitor gender policies usually have names referring to women. They are called 'Department for Women', 'Women's Equity Bureau', 'Prefectural Women's Centre' or 'Commission on the Status of Women'. Such bodies have a clear mandate to act for women. They do not have an equally clear mandate to act with respect to men. The major policy documents concerned with gender equality, such as the 1979 UN *Convention on the Elimination of all forms of Discrimination Against Women*, often do not name men as a group and rarely discuss men in concrete terms.

However, men are present as background throughout these documents. In every statement about women's disadvantage there is an implied comparison with men as the advantaged group. In the discussions of violence against women, men are implied and sometimes named as the perpetrators. In discussions of gender and HIV/AIDS, men are commonly construed as being the problem, the agents of infection.

When men are present only as a background category in a policy discourse about women, it is difficult to raise issues about men's and boys' interests, problems or diversity. This could only be done by falling into a backlash posture and affirming 'men's rights' or by moving outside a gender framework altogether.

The structure of gender equality policy, therefore, created an opportunity for anti-feminist politics. Opponents of feminism found issues about boys and men to be fertile ground. This is most clearly seen in the United States, where authors such as Christina Hoff Sommers (2000), purporting to defend men and boys, bitterly accused feminism of injustice. These ideas have not stimulated a social movement, with the exception of a small-scale (though active and sometimes violent) 'father's rights' movement in relation to divorce. The arguments have, however, strongly appealed to the neoconservative mass media, which gave them international circulation.

Some policymakers have attempted to straddle this divide by re-shaping gender equality policy as parallel policies for women and men. For instance, some health policymakers in Australia added a 'men's health' document to a 'women's health' document (Schofield 2004). Similarly, in some school systems a 'boy's education' strategy has been added to a 'girls' education' strategy (Lingard 2003).

This acknowledges the wider scope of gender issues. But this approach risks weakening the equality rationale of the original policy. It forgets the relational character of gender and therefore tends to redefine women and men, or girls and boys, simply as different market segments for some service. Ironically, the result may be to promote more gender segregation, not less.

On the other hand, bringing men's problems within an existing framework of policies for women may weaken the authority that women have so far gathered in that policy area. In the field of gender and development, for instance, some specialists argue that 'bringing men in' – given the larger context in which men still control most of the wealth and institutional authority – may undermine, not help, the drive for gender equality (White 2000).

The role of men and boys in relation to gender equality emerged as an issue in international discussions during the 1990s (Valdés and Olavarría 1998; Breines, Connell and Eide 2000). The shift became visible at the Fourth World Conference on Women, held in Beijing in 1995. Paragraph 25 of the *Beijing Declaration* committed participating governments to 'encourage men to participate fully in all actions towards equality'. The detailed *Platform for Action* that accompanied the Declaration prominently restated the principle of shared power and responsibility between men and women, and argued that women's concerns could only be addressed 'in partnership with men' towards gender equality (pars. 1, 3). The *Platform for Action* went on to specify areas where action involving men and boys was needed and was possible: in education, socialization of children, childcare and housework, sexual health, gender-based violence and the balancing of work and family reponsibilities (pars. 40, 72, 83b, 107c, 108e, 120, 179).

Participating governments followed a similar approach in the twenty-third special session of the UN General Assembly in the year 2000, which was intended to review the situation five years after the highly divided Beijing conference. The *Political Declaration* of this session made an even stronger statement on men's responsibility: '[Member states of the United Nations] emphasize that men must involve themselves and take joint responsibility with women for the promotion of gender equality' (par. 6). It remained the case that men were on the margins of a policy discourse concerned with women. The initiative of 2003–4 was an attempt to change this situation, to bring men's role in gender equality politics right into focus.

Divided interests: support and resistance

There is something surprising about the worldwide problematizing of men and masculinities, because in many ways the position of men has not much changed. Men remain a very large majority of corporate executives, top professionals and holders of public office. Worldwide, men hold nine out of ten cabinet-level posts in national governments, nearly as many of the parliamentary seats and most top positions in international agencies. Men, collectively, receive approximately twice the income that women receive and also receive the benefits of a great deal of unpaid household labour, not to mention emotional support, from women.

The United Nations Development Programme now regularly incorporates a selection of such statistics into its annual report on world human development, combining them into a 'gender-related development index' and a 'gender empowerment measure'. This produces a dramatic outcome, a league table of countries ranked in terms of gender equality, which shows most countries in the world to be far from gender-equal. It is clear that, globally, men have a lot to lose from pursuing gender equality because men, collectively, continue to receive a patriarchal dividend.

But this way of picturing inequality may conceal as much as it reveals. There are multiple dimensions in gender relations and the patterns of inequality in these dimensions may be different. If we look separately at each of the substructures of gender, we find a pattern of advantages for men but also a linked pattern of disadvantages or toxicity (Connell 2003a).

For instance, in relation to the gender division of labour, men collectively receive the bulk of income in the money economy, and men occupy most of the managerial positions. But men also provide the workforce for the most dangerous occupations, suffer most industrial injuries, pay most of the taxation, and are under heavier social pressure to remain employed. In the domain of power, men collectively control the institutions of coercion and the means of violence. But men are also the main targets of military violence and criminal assault, and many more men than women are imprisoned or executed.

One could draw up a balance sheet of the costs and benefits to men from the current gender order. But this would be misleading. The disadvantages are, broadly speaking, the *conditions* of the advantages. For instance, men cannot hold state power without some men becoming the agents of violence. Men cannot be the beneficiaries of women's domestic labour and care work without many men losing intimate connections with young children. Equally important, the men who receive most of the benefits, and the men who pay most of the costs, are not the same individuals. As the old saying puts it, generals die in bed. On a global scale, the men who benefit from corporate wealth, physical security and expensive health care are a very different group from the men who dig the fields and the mines of developing countries. Class, race, national, regional and generational differences cross-cut the category 'men', spreading the gains and costs of gender relations very unevenly among men. It is not surprising that men respond very diversely to gender equality politics.

There is, in fact, a considerable history of support for gender equality among men. Nineteenth-century intellectuals from Said Ahmad Khan in India to John Stuart Mill in Britain advocated the education and emancipation of women. Many of the historic gains by women's movements have been won in alliance with men who held organizational or political authority at the time. For instance, the introduction of Equal Employment Opportunity measures in New South Wales, Australia, occurred with the strong support of the Premier and the head of a reform inquiry into the public sector, both men (Eisenstein 1996).

The most prominent examples of organized pro-equality activism among men are concerned with gender-based violence. The White Ribbon campaign, conducting public education among men and boys, originated in Canada but is now international. Beginning in the 1990s, there are now research and action campaigns on the issue of violence in many countries (e.g. India: Chopra 2002). Since 2004 an international network called MenEngage, based on NGOs and UN agencies, has linked campaigns in many countries; over 400 organizations are now members.

What of the wider state of opinion? European survey research has shown no consensus among men either for or against gender equality. Sometimes a third/third/third pattern appears, with about one-third of men supporting change towards equality, about one-third opposing it and one-third undecided or intermediate

(Holter 1997: 131–4). Nevertheless, survey evidence from the United States, Germany and Japan does show a long-term trend of growing support for gender equality, especially among the younger generation (Mohwald 2002).

There is also significant evidence of men's and boys' *resistance* to change in gender relations. The survey research reveals substantial levels of doubt and opposition, especially among older men. Research on workplaces and on corporate management has documented many cases where men maintain an organizational culture that is heavily masculinized and unwelcoming to women. In some cases there is active opposition to gender equality measures or quiet undermining of them (Collinson and Hearn 1996). Research on schools has also found cases where boys assert control of informal social life and direct hostility against girls and against boys perceived as being different (Holland, Ramazanoglu, Sharpe and Thomson 1998).

Some men accept change in principle, but in practice still act in ways that sustain gender inequalities. In strongly gender-segregated societies it may be difficult for men to recognize alternatives or to understand women's experiences (Kandiyoti 1994; Fuller 2001; Meuser 2003). Another type of opposition to reform, more common among men in business and government, rejects gender equality measures because it rejects all government action in support of equality, in favour of the unfettered action of the market.

The reasons for men's resistance include the patriarchal dividend discussed above, and threats to identity that occur with change. If social definitions of masculinity emphasize being the breadwinner and being 'strong', then men may be offended by women's professional progress because it makes men seem less worthy of respect.

Resistance may also mean ideological defence of male supremacy. Research on domestic violence suggests that male batterers often hold very conservative views of women's role in the family (Ptacek 1988). In many parts of the world there are ideologies that justify men's supremacy on grounds of religion, biology, cultural tradition or organizational mission (e.g. in military forces). It is a mistake to regard these ideas as simply 'traditional' and therefore outmoded. They may be actively modernized and renewed.

Grounds for optimism

The public debates about men and boys have often been inconclusive. But they have gone a long way, together with the research, to shatter one widespread belief that has hindered gender reform. This is the belief that men *cannot* change their ways, that 'boys will be boys', that rape, sexism, brutality and selfishness are natural to men.

We now have many documented examples of the diversity of masculinities and of men's and boys' capacity for equality. For instance, life-history research in Chile has shown that there is no unitary Chilean masculinity. While a hegemonic model is widely diffused across social strata, there are many men who depart from it and there is significant discontent with traditional roles (Valdés and Olavarría 1998).

Though boys in schools often have a dominant or hegemonic pattern of masculinity, there are usually also other patterns present, some of which involve more equal and respectful relations with girls. There is very interesting research in Britain, for instance, that shows how boys encounter and explore alternative models of masculinity as they grow up (Mac an Ghaill 1994; O'Donnell and Sharpe 2000).

Psychological and educational research shows personal flexibility in the face of gender stereotypes. Men and boys can strategically use conventional definitions of masculinity, rather than being rigidly dominated by them. It is even possible to teach boys (and girls) how to do this in school, as experiments in Australian classrooms have shown (Davies 1993; Wetherell and Edley 1999).

Perhaps the most extensive social action involving men in gender change has occurred in Scandinavia. This includes provisions for paternity leave that have had high rates of take-up, among the most dramatic of all demonstrations of men's willingness to change gender practices. Øystein Holter sums up the research and practical experience in an important statement:

> The Nordic 'experiment' has shown that a *majority* of men can change their practice when circumstances are favourable . . . When reforms or support policies are well-designed and targeted towards an on-going cultural process of change, men's active support for gender-equal status increases. (Holter 2003: 126)

Many groups of men, it is clear, have a capacity for equality and for gender change. But what reasons for change are men likely to see?

Early statements often assumed that men had the same interest as women in escaping from restrictive sex roles (e.g. Palme 1972). Later experience has not confirmed this view. Yet men and boys often do have substantial reasons to support change.

First, men are not isolated individuals. Men and boys live in social relationships, many with women and girls: wives, partners, mothers, aunts, daughters, nieces, friends, classmates, workmates, professional colleagues, neighbours and so on. The quality of every man's life depends to a large extent on the quality of those relationships. We may therefore speak of men's *relational interests* in gender equality.

For instance, very large numbers of men are fathers and about half of their children are girls. Some men are sole parents and deeply involved in caregiving – an important demonstration of men's capacity for care (Risman 1986). Even in intact partnerships with women, many men have close relationships with their children, and psychological research shows the importance of these relationships (Kindler 2002). In several parts of the world, young men are exploring more engaged patterns of fatherhood (Olavarría 2001). To make sure that daughters grow up in a world that offers young women security, freedom and opportunities to fulfil their talents is a powerful reason for many men to support gender equality.

Second, men may wish to avoid the toxic effects that the gender order has for them. James Harrison (1978) long ago issued a 'Warning: The male sex role may be dangerous to your

health'. Since then, health research has documented specific problems for men and boys. Among them are premature death from
accident, homicide and suicide; occupational injury; higher levels
of drug abuse, especially of alcohol and tobacco; in some countries, a relative unwillingness by men to seek medical help when
it is needed. Attempts to assert a tough and dominant masculinity sustain some of these toxic practices (Hurrelmann and Kolip
2002).

Social and economic pressures on men to compete in the
workplace, to increase their hours of paid work and sometimes
to take second jobs, are among the most powerful constraints on
gender reform. Desire for a better balance between work and life
is widespread among employed men. On the other hand, where
unemployment is high, the lack of a paid job can be a damaging pressure on men who have grown up with the expectation
of being breadwinners. This is, for instance, an important gender
issue in post-Apartheid South Africa, where there is active discussion of new patterns of fatherhood (Richter and Morrell 2006).
Opening alternative economic paths and moving towards what
German discussions have called 'multi-optional masculinities'
may do much to improve men's well-being (Widersprüche 1998;
Morrell 2001a).

Third, men may support gender change because they see its
relevance to the well-being of the community they live in. In situations of mass poverty and under-employment, for instance cities
in developing countries, flexibility in the gender division of labour
may be crucial to a household's survival. Rahul Roy's recent film
City Beautiful provides a striking example of this dilemma for
working-class families in India.

Reducing the rigidity of masculinities may also yield benefits in
security. Gender relations are, as Cynthia Cockburn (2010) argues,
causally related to militarization and war. Men as well as women
have an interest in peace.

Finally, men may support gender reform because gender equality follows from their political or ethical principles. These may be
religious, socialist or broad democratic beliefs. J. S. Mill based the
case for gender equality on classical liberal principles; Ali Shariati

based the case for gender equality on Qur'anic principles. The idea of equal human rights still has credibility among large groups of men.

Grounds for pessimism

The diversity among men and masculinities is reflected in a diversity of men's movements. A study in the United States found multiple movements, with different agendas for the remaking of masculinity, operating on the terrains of gender equality, men's rights and ethnic or religious identities (Messner 1997). There is no unified political position for men and no authoritative representative of men's interests.

The most extensive experience of any group of men organizing around issues of gender and sexual politics is that of homosexual men – in antidiscrimination campaigns, the gay liberation movement and community responses to the HIV/AIDS pandemic. Gay men have pioneered in areas such as community care for the sick, community education for responsible sexual practices, representation in the public sector and overcoming social exclusion (Kippax *et al.* 1993; Altman 1994). Though tolerance has grown, homosexual men frequently face opposition and sometimes severe violence from other men.

Explicit 'backlash' movements exist, but have not generally had a great deal of influence. Men mobilizing as men to oppose women tend to be seen as cranks or fanatics. Much more important for the defence of gender inequality are movements and institutions in which men's interests are indirectly promoted – among them churches, ethnic organizations, conservative parties and nationalist movements.

A particularly important case of indirect gender politics is neoliberalism, the dominant economic ideology today. Neoliberalism is in principle gender neutral. The 'individual' has no gender, and the market delivers advantage to the smartest entrepreneur, not to men or women as such. But neoliberalism does not pursue social justice in relation to gender. In Eastern Europe the restoration of capitalism and the arrival of neoliberal politics were followed by a sharp deterioration in the position of women. In rich Western countries, neoliberalism from the 1980s on has attacked the welfare state, on which far more women than men depend; supported deregulation of labour markets, resulting in increased casualization of women workers; shrunk public sector employment, the sector of the economy where women predominate; lowered rates of personal taxation, the main basis of tax transfers to women; and squeezed public education, the key pathway to labour market advancement for women. However, the same period saw an expansion of the human-rights agenda, which is, on the whole, an asset for gender equality.

Neoliberalism can function as a form of masculinity politics largely because of the powerful role of the state in the gender order. The state constitutes gender relations in multiple ways and all of its gender policies affect men. Many mainstream policies (e.g. in economic and security affairs) are substantially about men or advance men's interests, without acknowledging this fact (Bezanson and Luxton 2006).

This points to a realm of institutional politics where men's and women's interests are very much at stake, without the publicity created by social movements. Public-sector agencies (Schofield and Goodwin 2005), private-sector corporations (Connell 2010), and unions (Franzway 2001) are all sites of masculinized power and struggles for gender equality. In each of these sites some men can be found with a commitment to gender equality, but in each case that is an embattled position. For gender-equality outcomes it is important to have support from men in the top organizational levels, but this is not often reliably forthcoming.

One reason for the difficulty in expanding men's opposition to sexism is the role of highly conservative men as cultural authorities and managers. Major religious organizations, in Christianity, Islam and Buddhism, are controlled by men who sometimes completely exclude women. The Catholic Church, for instance, vehemently refuses to have women as priests, and the Pope has recently denounced the very concept of 'gender'. Transnational media organizations, such as the Murdoch (Fox) media empire, are also active in promoting conservative gender ideology.

Men and men's interests are central in the growing complex of commercial sport. With its overwhelming focus on male athletes; its celebration of force, domination and competitive success; its valorization of male commentators and executives; and its marginalization and frequent ridicule of women, the sports/business complex has become an increasingly important site for representing and defining gender. This is not traditional patriarchy. It is something new, welding exemplary bodies to entrepreneurial culture. Michael Messner (2002), one of the leading sociologists of sport, formulates the effect well by saying that commercial sports define the renewed centrality of men and of a particular version of masculinity.

On a world scale, explicit backlash movements are of limited importance, but very large numbers of men are nevertheless engaged in preserving gender inequality. Patriarchy is defended diffusely. There is support for change from equally large numbers of men, but it is an uphill battle to articulate that support. That is the political context with which new gender-equality initiatives have to deal.

Ways forward: a global framework

Inviting men to end men's privileges and to remake masculinities to sustain gender equality, strikes many people as a strange or utopian project. Yet this project is already underway. Many men around the world are engaged in gender reforms, for the good reasons discussed above.

The diversity of masculinities complicates the process but is also an important asset. As this diversity becomes better known, men and boys can more easily see a range of possibilities for their own lives, while men and women are less likely to think of gender inequality as eternal. It also becomes possible to identify specific groups of men who might join in alliances for change.

Public policy for gender equality relies on the idea of an alliance between men and women. Some groups within the women's movement, especially those concerned with men's violence, are reluctant to work with men or are deeply sceptical of men's willingness to change. Other feminists argue that alliances between women and men are possible, even crucial. In some social movements, for instance environmentalism, there is a strong ideology of gender equality and a favourable environment for men to support gender change (Connell 2005a; Segal 1997).

In local and central government, practical alliances between women and men have been important in achieving reforms such as equal-opportunity hiring rules. Even in dealing with men's violence against women, there has been cooperation between women's groups and men's groups, for instance in prevention work. This cooperation can be an inspiration to grassroots workers and a powerful demonstration of women's and men's common interest in a peaceful and equal society (Pease 1997). The concept of alliance is itself important, in preserving autonomy for women's groups, in pre-empting a tendency for one group to speak for others, and in defining a political role for men that has some dignity and might attract widespread support.

Given the spectrum of masculinity politics, we cannot expect consensus for gender equality. What is possible is that support for gender equality might become hegemonic among men. In that case it would be groups supporting equality that provide the agenda for public discussion about men's lives and patterns of masculinity.

There is already a broad cultural shift towards a historical consciousness about gender, an awareness that gender customs came into existence at specific moments in time and can always be transformed by social action. What is needed now is a widespread sense of agency among men, a sense that this transformation is something they can actually share in as a practical proposition.

From this point of view, the 2004 meeting of the UN Commission on the Status of Women (CSW) was profoundly interesting. The CSW is one of the oldest of UN agencies, dating from the 1940s. Effectively a standing committee of the General Assembly, it meets annually and its practice has been to consider two main themes at each meeting. For the 2004 meeting, one of the defined themes was 'the role of men and boys in achieving gender equality'. The section of the UN secretariat that supports the CSW, the Division for the Advancement of Women, undertook background work. The Division held, in June–July 2003, a worldwide online seminar on the role of men and boys, and in October 2003 it convened an international expert group meeting in Brasilia on the topic.

At the main CSW meetings, there is a presentation of the Division's background work, and delegations of the forty-five current member countries, UN agencies and many of the nongovernment organizations attending make initial statements. There is a busy schedule of side events, mainly organized by NGOs but some conducted by delegations or UN agencies. And there is a diplomatic process, in which the official delegations negotiate over a draft document in the light of discussions in the CSW and their governments' stances on gender issues.

This is a politicized process, inevitably, and it can break down. In 2003, the CSW discussion on the issue of violence against women reached deadlock. In 2004 it was clear that some participating NGOs were not happy with the focus on men and boys, some holding to a discourse about men exclusively as perpetrators of violence. Over the two weeks of negotiations, however, the delegations did reach consensus on a policy statement, known as 'Agreed Conclusions'.

Reaffirming commitment to women's equality and recognizing men's and boys' potential for action, this document made specific recommendations across policy fields such as education, parenthood, media, the labour market, sexuality, violence and conflict prevention. These proposals have no force in international law – the document is essentially a set of recommendations to governments and other organizations. Nevertheless, it was the first international agreement of its kind, treating men systematically as agents in gender-equality processes. It created a standard for future gender-equality discussions, presenting gender equality as a positive project for men.

An account of these discussions and examples of action projects around the world is now available in a widely distributed document *The Role of Men and Boys in Achieving Gender Equality* (Division for the Advancement of Women 2008).

The United Nations process connects with the social and cultural possibilities that have emerged from the last three decades of gender politics among men. Gender equality is an undertaking for men that can be creative and joyful. It is a project that realizes high principles of social justice, produces better lives for the women whom men care about, and will produce better lives for the majority of men in the long run. This can and should be a project that generates energy, that finds expression in everyday life and the arts as well as in formal policies, that can illuminate all aspects of men's lives.

2

Steering towards Equality? How Gender Regimes Change inside the State

It is a truth universally acknowledged that we live in an era of gender change. Gender identities, gender performance and gender relations are all supposed to be in flux. Mr Bingley, though in possession of a good fortune, may no longer be in want of a wife.

Whether the process of gender change can be *steered*, in the sense of following a conscious agenda of reform, is an important and difficult question. Gender equality policies are precisely an attempt to do this. Neoliberals broadly assume that 'social engineering' is impossible or wrong. Feminists debate how to steer gender change and how to evaluate the experience of those who have tried (Eisenstein 2009).

This argument centres on the main steering mechanism in modern societies, the state. A considerable volume of feminist research has shown how state agencies and policies regulate the lives of women, both in the family and in the public realm (Borchorst 1999). The research focus has widened to the state's influence on gender relations generally, including the gendered lives of men (Connell 2003b).

In early discussions of the patriarchal state it was common

to speak as if 'the state' were a single unit. But actual states are complex agglomerations of agencies, differing along gender lines and often pursuing different agendas. The state's impact on gender relations will depend partly on what is happening *inside* state agencies. We know, since the work of Joan Acker (1990) and Clare Burton (1987), that organizations themselves are bearers of gender relations. Every organization can be characterized through its gender regime, i.e. the pattern of gender relations that structures the gender practices of its participants.

We also know that state agencies are not static as organizations. Indeed they have been flooded by structural change. Corporatization and privatization of public sector agencies, 'welfare reform' and the 'new public management' are the most visible elements of a broad reform agenda. And as Anna Yeatman (1990) pointed out, there is an interplay between gender reform and other agendas of change in state institutions.

Taken as a whole, research shows that state agencies have two connections to the steering of gender change. They are engaged through their being *state* agencies, that is bearers of legal and financial powers in relation to the society they act upon. But they are also engaged through their being state *agencies*, that is organizations with their own gender regimes, gender dynamics and other patterns of change.

To understand how this double relationship works and what its strategic implications are, it is essential to understand how change in gender relations is experienced within state agencies. This is not easy to know. Much of the research consists of statistical data about the numbers of women and men in different organizational slots. This reveals broad trends, but not the mechanisms underlying them, nor the complexities within them. On the other hand, close-focus case studies leave the reader uncertain how widespread the mechanisms and complexities are.

This chapter tries to bridge the gap. It reports findings from multiple case studies, conducted in a common format, within a larger research program that gave information about the sector as a whole. The Gender Equity in Public Institutions (GEPI) project was a large research programme conducted by a team from the

University of Sydney and the NSW public sector. Part of the project was a field study that examined the gender regimes of specific worksites in five agencies.

The agencies included both 'central' and 'line' agencies, covered a variety of industries and governmental functions, and varied markedly in size. In each agency one site concerned with central administration or policymaking was chosen, plus another more directly concerned with operations or service delivery.

The fieldwork was done from May 2001 to October 2002. 107 focused interviews were completed and transcribed. They covered four dimensions of gender relations – power and authority, divisions of labour, emotional relations, and culture and communication (Connell 2009). They also explored gender equity programs, work/life balance and career patterns. The interviewing emphasized practices and experiences, not just attitudes. Most interviews lasted between 40 and 80 minutes. With the agreement of the respondents, interviews were tape-recorded. As the gender balance in small worksites varies widely, no attempt was made to interview equal numbers of women and men in each site, but some men and some women were interviewed at each site, overall totals being 58 women and 49 men. In two sites, a researcher also spent approximately three weeks as a participant observer.

The transcripts went through a careful process of analysis, designed to deepen understanding of the sites and avoid idiosyncratic interpretations. Each interview was abstracted and indexed, following a plan based on the conceptual framework. The same indexing plan was applied to the field notes from participant observation. For each of the ten sites, a full-scale case study was then written. Draft site reports were discussed with representatives of the agencies concerned, to correct errors, and then workshopped by the project steering committee. In these meetings, comparisons across sites began to emerge. A general report on the study was then written and this too was workshopped with the agency representatives.

Times of change

Participants from all sites were aware of living in a time of change. Older staff especially had a strong sense of 'then' and 'now' in the broad gender patterns of society. When they were young, the usual account ran, women's job expectations were extremely limited, all bosses were men, education was mostly segregated, women had to wear skirts to work and had to flirt to get what they wanted. A woman from a central office in a human services agency recalls, as many of the older women did:

> I did . . . a secretarial course, because I didn't know what I wanted to do. And my Mum said, Well if you can do shorthand and typing you'll always be able to get a job . . . I didn't think I was going to end up being a secretary and doing secretarial stuff all my life. But I couldn't think what else to do.

Now young women can. Women's job opportunities are seen as more diverse, women are much freer to express themselves, there are women in powerful positions, men are more likely to help with housework, there is less harassment and open sexism. To many of our participants, Australian society in the past generation has gone from being highly segregated and hierarchical in gender terms to being much more integrated and much more equal.

Many participants described a change inside the public sector that corresponded to this larger picture of social change. They observed that women's employment is now diverse, job ghettoes such as the typing pool have disappeared, women are now present in management, dress codes are more relaxed and 'boys' clubs' are in decline. In short, many worksites in the NSW public sector have been de-gendered. Old occupational barriers have been removed and physical segregation of men and women has ended.

In some cases this de-gendering is clearly connected with a change in the labour process and the organizational structure. Two of the study sites were in an infrastructure agency where a traditional form of heavy and dirty labour by blue-collar men has been automated over the last decade. This agency's workforce has been drastically down-sized. With a new labour process centring on computer control systems, old occupational divisions have collapsed. A new integrated occupational category has been created which is open to women as well as to men. At the same time, a multi-layered bureaucratic hierarchy has been simplified into a 'flat' structure, with the basis of authority shifting from seniority to professional qualifications. Both changes have undermined the organizational power of old styles of masculinity that are familiar in engineering and heavy industry (Donaldson 1991).

A change almost as profound has occurred in office work. Since all public sector agencies have offices, this change occurs in all participating agencies and the majority of specific sites. The old labour process centred on producing and filing paper documents: letters, file cards, minutes and so on. A category of workers who were mostly women (typists and secretaries) produced, filed and retrieved documents, on the instructions of managers and professionals who were mostly men.

The advent of word-processing, data banks and email since the 1970s has changed this. The typing pool has been abolished. The secretary and the filing clerk have mostly gone (partly replaced by the 'personal assistant', but this is likely to be a young person getting experience rather than a woman in a lifetime job). Managers and professionals do much of their own keyboard work. In one of the sites, part of a central agency, our researcher conducted participant observation in a room where a mixed group of administrators, sitting at closely packed workstations, spent hours each day staring at their individual computer screens. In a sense this is a gender-blending scene. Labour that was formerly coded masculine (administrative) has been combined with labour formerly coded feminine (secretarial) in the same job.

Changes of this kind have called patterns of middle-class masculinity into question. The old hierarchical structures called for certain qualities. The 'good bureaucrat' could be defined (to synthesize remarks from different participants) as hard-working, loyal to the organization, respectful of seniority, patient about climbing the ladder and scrupulous about due process. He was able to give and receive clear instructions, he was concerned for the public interest, knowledgeable about the specific field in which his department worked and knowledgeable about the public sector scene as a whole. A marriage and a supportive wife were more or less assumed.

Public service reform has opened up the world in which this model of bureaucratic masculinity was hegemonic. Not all our respondents are impressed with the results. The phrase 'good bureaucrat' comes from a participant who thinks that public sector change has given leadership roles to people who:

> aren't really anything like the calibre of the good bureaucrats that were around previously.

There is certainly a shift in the characteristics expected of managers, a change that appears across most sites and all agencies. As described by managers themselves, the work now emphasizes consultation, negotiation, networking, circulating information, forming teams, facilitating and encouraging the work of others. It is less rule-bound, more fluid. Concern with rules is to some extent replaced by entrepreneurship and inventiveness. Patience and seniority are replaced by networking and career planning; issuing instructions is replaced by persuasion and communication; and specific administrative knowledge is replaced by generic management skills. This is a formula that women can be seen to match and some of our respondents believe that women are *better* than men at certain parts of the package.

However, a more fluid labour process can more readily be intensified. This too is seen across a range of sites in the study. The managers are subject to intense (though fluctuating) time pressure. They often have to work late, often have to meet short deadlines. Therefore the new public sector management, while officially de-gendered, in practice is likely to continue the strongly gendered work/home imbalance described by Judy Wajcman (1999) for the private sector. The key gender divide has shifted slightly. Rather than running between women and men, it now runs between women with children, and men plus women without childcare responsibilities (or women who can pass on their childcare responsibilities).

In other respects too, the picture of growing gender integration must be qualified. In the infrastructure agency mentioned above, some participants warned us not to exaggerate the picture of change. Despite all the reforms, this agency still mainly employs men. In one of the human service agencies, the researchers met a group of workers doing routine keyboard work, data entry and retrieval from a database. They were all women. This was one of the most gender-segregated workplaces in the whole study. In both these cases a pattern of gender segregation has survived the technical transformation of the labour process. This is a useful warning not to overstate the direct impact of 'technology' in transforming gender, a point strongly made by Wajcman (2004).

In other sites, women participants point to continuing sexism, both inside and outside the public sector, and mention arrogant and oppressive men still there in management. Beyond the workplace, for many public sector workers, family divisions of labour have changed very little. Women still provide the bulk of childcare and domestic services and men consume the services.

To summarize: change in gender patterns is experienced as a fact of everyday working life across the NSW public sector, at all levels from manual labour to policy work. Relatively widespread changes include the automation of masculinized industrial labour, the transformation of clerical work and the disappearance of the 'secretary', and the growing fluidity of managerial labour. These changes, however, are uneven from site to site. They fall far short of complete de-gendering or equality. At the grassroots worksite level, the agencies in the study remain gendered institutions.

Gender as a problem in organizational life – and a non-problem

In thinking about new directions for gender equity policy, as Carol Bacchi and Joan Eveline (2010) argue, it is important to know how gender gets recognized as a problem that organizations still need to address. In some of our study sites there were organizational problems that were clearly recognized as gender issues. Most fall into three types.

The first concerns men, either individuals or groups, who have difficulty accepting the gender changes occurring in their workplaces. Especially they had difficulty with the arrival of women in roles other than traditional support roles. In one service delivery site there had been considerable conflict of this kind. Management had banned pornography, brought women into all-male workplaces, banned harassment and so on. In some units of this agency a marked shift towards cooperative gender relations had occurred. In other units there was little change. The men evidently saw the work as wrong for women or saw women as intruders in a masculine domain. Women were seen as creating embarrassment and difficulty, disrupting the solidarity of work units and not having the skills, strength or commitment needed for the work. Even in units where women and men now combined successfully as a group, some individual men maintained their opposition.

The second recognized problem concerns women managers. Though the principle of women holding management positions is now uncontestable, in practice women's authority may be contested, challenged, ignored or doubted in many ways. For instance, a female manager in one of our agencies was treated with scorn by a male colleague of equal rank. He belittled her proposals in meetings and behind her back, and refused to communicate with her, until obliged to go into a mediation process. In another site, a male worker would not accept direction from a female supervisor, always going over her head to get instructions confirmed by a male superior. In a third case, a much-restructured site in a regulatory agency, women are now prominent in senior management. But they are thought by some of the workforce, especially men, to have been promoted too fast and therefore to lack skill and background.

The emotion in these disputes is significant. It is difficult to quote examples because specific people may be identifiable, but the tone is conveyed by one man's story about another agency, outside the study:

I notice that especially women who get into senior positions, the first thing they want to do is to exert their authority . . . They've appointed a woman over there as the director of [Unit], now she has gone totally feral. She has told him to, you know, 'Get fucked, you're useless, I have been carrying you since I got here.' And it just degenerated. Luckily she said it in front of another person . . . and that was the culmination of about six or eight months of just abuse and bullying.

There are enough such comments – some more hostile than that – to indicate a continuing problem in establishing women's authority in management. At the same time, we encountered a number of situations, sometimes in the same agencies, where women managers *were* accepted and respected by their workforces. There is not a blanket rejection by men.

The third issue concerns participants, in a number of sites, who feel they or their colleagues have suffered gender discrimination. This complaint is made by men as well as by women. There is however a difference in what they complain about. The women are complaining about old-fashioned harassment and sexism. Examples are misogynist jokes (updated in one respect: they now come by email), being felt up, being stared at, their bodies and appearance commented upon, and not being taken seriously as co-workers. The men who complain of discrimination feel they are up against something new and even sinister. They believe that their manager is a feminist who has something to prove against men, that there is an organized push to get women into top jobs, that they are '*victims of the sisterhood*' as a male respondent (who distanced himself from these claims) put it. These complaints are noticeably less specific than the women's complaints, but strong feelings are clearly involved.

It was easy for the researchers to identify these gender problems. Yet when asked what current gender problems existed in their workplace, most participants, in most sites, reported that there were few or none. In some cases the answer went further and respondents praised the workplace for gender sensitivity and positive relations between women and men. Other sites were characterized as peaceful workplaces, with no open conflicts and no sexual harassment. This also seems an important finding. For much of the time, across much of the public sector, gender is regarded as a non-problem.

This was not because participants were unable to 'see' gender issues at all. The same people often did comment on gender problems – but located them *elsewhere*. Gender conflicts were located in the past, in an organizational history that has now been transcended. Or they were located in other units, in other agencies or in other sectors of society. Here for instance is a woman who works at the policy-advice level in a central agency:

> Not in this workplace, it is obvious, you just have to look around, there is so many women . . . So I can't see any problem. I get along well with, it is a very cooperative [unit] to work in, people are quite prepared to share their knowledge and their experience whether male or female. So I have never encountered any chauvinism if I can put it that way, you know, where you are locked out. I have experienced it in the past . . . When you're developing policy, gender doesn't really have a role to play in my view.

We were also told of many episodes that were seen as gender problems, but were not seen as *organizational* gender problems. For instance, sexist comments from a man were often discussed by a woman as a problem about a prejudiced individual. Here is an example from an infrastructure agency:

> There is a few people here, a few men here, who still have that, you know, real sort of 'How are you darling?', 'How is it going?', pat on the bum, really male chauvinistic, sexual overtones in everything they say. And it is just a pain in the arse. They're not senior managers or anything like that, it is just the staff.

A good deal of gender trouble is handled informally at an individual level. In this site, for instance, women express confidence in their ability to handle sexist behaviour from such men, now that the gross sexism of the old work culture has mostly gone. The woman just quoted went on to describe how she dealt with criticism from a male manager about participating in a women's staff development program:

> I wouldn't take any crap when he made a comment, I told him where to go with it – not quite that way, but you know, I pretty much set him straight. And it is funny because he has never said anything to me since.

The fact that gender equity and anti-discrimination are now official policy may result, ironically, in unwillingness to articulate gender problems. A sexist comment from a man may be judged by a woman far too small an issue to call the anti-discrimination machinery into play. When this is put together with tendencies to play down the gender dimension of problems, to speak of gender-related issues as personal 'choices' (especially work/life balance issues) and to step cautiously in personal interactions, we get a picture of an almost subterranean gender politics in organizational life. Indeed a thoughtful participant spoke of gender being '*increasingly disguised*' in the life of the agency, despite having real effects.

The direction of change – towards the gender-neutral workplace

The picture of broad gender change is taken by some participants as an indication that the reform agenda has succeeded. A middle-aged man sums up his experience of change:

> I would like to think we are a little bit more enlightened now. I think it has been proven that women can do just about any job that a male can do, that there is no male-dominated industries as such – maybe the construction industry is. But I think that from an Agency viewpoint and even from a workplace viewpoint now, it is accepted that we have got women [professional staff], they can come in and do just as good a job as what men can do.

This is correct, in the sense that there is hardly any occupation, industry or organizational level from which women are now entirely absent. As our site studies show, some of the most gender-typed occupations have been practically abolished or opened to all comers. Some formerly gender-coded forms of work have been blended to form gender-integrated labour processes.

But where is this change heading? The younger participants have a sense that things were different once, but have less sense of gender struggle. Among the younger women in professional or administrative jobs, there is often a sense that gender inequality has completely gone. Some remark that they have never experienced gender discrimination, deny that there is a 'glass ceiling' and construct their career plans in the expectation of rising to the top on the same terms as men.

This connects to the 'not a gender issue' theme mentioned in the last section. One participant described how a task in her regulatory agency was done differently by a mostly male work group and an all-female work group; then hastened to add that this wasn't *'because they were male . . . it wasn't a gender thing'* – it was just a preference! A younger man from the same site, asked about the local state of gender relations, replied:

> I don't really care if a person is a man or woman . . . [and] if a man and a woman don't like each other, it is nothing to do with their sex, it is just personality difference, you know.

There is something here that goes beyond underplaying gender issues. There is a rejection of even the possibility of gender discord, of divergent interests or practices. There is a distinct element of gender *denial* in some current discourse.

Gender neutrality can also be seen as an ethical ideal. This view was put eloquently by a senior woman in a human services agency:

> The day that dawns that gender is not an issue and people are accepted for what they are and who they are, in their glorious individuality, is where we would hope to be.

What is common to these statements is the implicit goal of a *gender-neutral workplace*. On the evidence of this study, the idea of gender neutrality has to a significant extent displaced 'gender equality' or 'women's advancement' as the guiding idea of gender reform. Gender neutrality is pursued in a range of ways: equal-opportunity recruitment practices, the definition of jobs, the geography of the office, the dress code, even a shared style of speech – task-focused and professional. Across sites, the new style of management also reinforces gender neutrality. The shift from a hierarchical, rule-bound, seniority-obsessed managerial system to a more entrepreneurial model that emphasizes networking and negotiation has broken down an old model of bureaucratic masculinity, sometimes in the very recent history of these agencies.

The new management model is in turn supported by the rise of an individualist view of the world. In the neoliberal outlook, differences in people's situations or actions are essentially the outcomes of the choices they have made as individuals. Thus 'it wasn't a gender thing', it was just a preference. It is easy to see how young professionally qualified women in a corporatized agency may simply deny that any glass ceiling exists and expect to make their own individual ways into an open-ended future.

Reflections

The equal-opportunity reform efforts of the last generation have had an important impact on public sector life. Pathways have been opened for women, sexist organizational cultures have been challenged and some questions about men and masculinity have been raised. As participants see it, these changes have been part of a wider readjustment in the lives of women and men. Nevertheless the change has not been uniform nor smooth. This study provides abundant evidence of the unevenness and sometimes turbulence of gender changes within the state apparatus.

In several sites in the study, the transformation of an old gender division of labour and the breakdown of old gender hierarchies has occurred with re-structures: 'flat' organization, re-engineering of labour processes and amalgamation of occupations. Re-structures do not necessarily transform gender relations. It is clear in some of our sites that gender divisions have survived organizational surgery. But the upheavals probably made it easier to carry through a gender reform program, if there was also the political will.

The new style of public sector management is self-consciously gender-inclusive and it values skills traditionally seen as feminine, such as abilities to communicate, empathize and support. It is also much more individualist than old-style management, in accord with neoliberal views of organizational life. From such a perspective, the idea of a gender-neutral workplace provides an acceptable resolution of the dilemmas around gender equity.

Yet gender neutrality is hard to achieve in practice – or is perhaps assumed to exist where it actually does not. In some sites we saw strong gender divisions of labour and we could see, at the point of entry to occupations, strong gender divisions being reproduced for the next generation. In other sites we met more moderate concentrations of men and women that still reflected a tendency towards division.

It is not just a matter of persisting tradition; *new* gender divisions of labour come into existence. Among the most gender-segregated units we encountered were places where data entry into massive databanks was occurring and where all-woman groups of workers were doing routine, fairly boring work with few promotion prospects. Here was new technology and new labour process, but in other respects the picture was very like the typing pools of the past.

Beyond all this is the gender division of labour in households, which remains intransigent. Its impact on women and men in the public sector, as in the private sector, is profound. The domestic division of labour sharply undermines the gender-neutrality of new public sector management. The tendency for the labour process of management to expand indefinitely makes the ability to commit unlimited time to the organization a key requirement for being an effective manager and positioning oneself for promotion. As in private sector management, this is very much easier for people with wives.

Here the state's double engagement in gender change, as the means of social steering but also as an arena of change, comes into focus. The sense of 'gender elsewhere', noted earlier, is partly produced by looking out from a state agency where gender neutrality is assumed, towards a social world where gender neutrality is very definitely not a reality.

Public sector workers are often dealing with gender relations in the world outside. Examples are police intervening in domestic disputes, industrial tribunals enforcing equal pay, schools dealing with subject choices and sexual harassment among pupils, and welfare agencies dealing with gendered poverty. For three of our ten sites such matters are major issues, and most of the other sites deal with gender questions to some extent.

Thus gender problems generated outside the walls become part of public sector agencies' business. The gender relations encountered this way are sometimes oppressive, the problems messy, the conflicts difficult to resolve. Like the issue of the domestic division of labour, these are matters where the idea of a gender-neutral organization provides very little guidance.

The more that the neoliberal perspective becomes dominant, the more difficult it becomes to justify any equity measure which does not consist of multiplying 'choices'. The idea of a gender-neutral workplace is highly acceptable because it is the only way of reconciling the principle of gender equality with the framework of neoliberal thought. In the gender-neutral workplace, everyone is free to choose, not as men and women, but as individuals. That there are people who have no room to choose or whose choices have effectively been made for them and who therefore need structural solutions to an equity problem – such an idea can hardly arise.

So an important difficulty for gender equality policy is created by the current pattern of organizational change. As gender equality policy increasingly focuses on creating a gender-neutral workplace, it *reduces* the steering capacity of the state to contribute to gender equality in society.

We are not at a point where all other possibilities are dead. The fieldwork found sites where gender equality principles are strongly embedded in organizational culture. This was particularly the case where broad equity principles accompanied commitment to an idea of public service. Belief in *public service* as an ethical ground of public sector work, rather than performativity, is one of the most powerful hidden assets of modern government. It operates, in one form or another, in many of the sites in this study and in some cases it was very impressive to see.

This ethic, however, is at risk from the market agenda. Struggle over gender issues in the public sector is by no means ended. It seems, however, likely to take new shapes in the future, with the steering capacity of the state itself at stake.

3

The Neoliberal Parent: Mothers and Fathers in Market Society

The family is often imagined as the most stable of all our social institutions, the anchor of identity and the rock on which social order is built. Yet we know that families change over time. Large-scale social transformations such as colonialism, industrialization, mass migration and war have all impacted on family relationships.

In this chapter I consider the most recent of these historic changes, the worldwide creation of a neoliberal economic/political regime. By 'neoliberalism' I mean the project of transformation under the sign of the free market that has dominated politics in the last quarter-century, both in the global metropole (western Europe and north America) and in most other parts of the world.

Neoliberalism is most familiar as a set of economic policies and supporting ideas. The 'free market' is the central image and deregulation measures that were supposed to free the markets, especially capital markets, were among the earliest and most important neoliberal policies.

Neoliberalism seeks to make existing markets wider and to create new markets where they did not exist before. Neoliberalism pushes towards the universal commodification of services. The most dramatic form is the privatization of public assets such as land, railways and electricity. However neoliberals have been quite inventive in finding ways to commodify public services as well. For instance, private schools are subsidized and public universities are forced to charge fees. Social welfare is commodified by putting the provision of social services up for tender and forcing the public agencies that formerly provided them to compete with NGOs and companies to win the tenders.

Cutting taxes remains an important part of neoliberal rhetoric. Neoliberal policies have halted the growth of public sector expenditure, which translates into a real squeeze on many public services. This gradual process in the economies of the metropole was packaged in a more drastic form in the IMF 'Structural Adjustment Programs' of the 1980s and 1990s imposed on countries of the periphery.

In the remaining public sector, a new ethos of managerialism appears. Managers' salaries and bonuses rise, in both the private and the public sector, to unprecedented levels. An emphasis on labour market flexibility produces a growing workforce of part-time and casual and contract labour at the bottom of the organizations. Applying market discipline to the labour force has meant sustained pressure against unions. There has been an irregular but insistent roll-back of entitlements and security which the organized part of the working class had historically won.

Thus neoliberalism has succeeded in changing the connection between politics and economy in much of the world. In the metropole, it has dismantled the Keynesian welfare state, the system of regulated capitalism and state-supplied services that was dominant in the generation from 1945 to 1980. In the global periphery, neoliberalism has dismantled the social-democratic developmentalist state and broken up the social alliances around it – most successfully in Latin America, Africa and Oceania.

The forces driving neoliberalism are generally understood through a systems model of capitalism. To David Harvey (2005), for instance, neoliberalism is the rationalization of a late stage of capitalism, to be explained through the current need for 'flexible accumulation'. In Gérard Duménil and Dominique Lévy's *Capital Resurgent* (2004), neoliberalism is finance capital's response to a crisis of profitability that emerged in the world's dominant economies in the late 1960s and 1970s. There is much in these arguments; but they are too narrow. They locate the driving force of neoliberalism inside the global metropole. But the first country to adopt a strongly neoliberal economic regime, in the 1970s, was Chile. It was in New Zealand and Australia that labour governments in the 1980s pioneered the shift from social democracy to neoliberalism. In the 1990s the great triumph of neoliberalism was in the former Soviet bloc. And since 2000 it has been Latin America where the most powerful contestation of neoliberalism has emerged, from social movements and governments. With Samir Amin (1997), I consider that neoliberalism has as much to do with the restructuring of metropole/periphery relations as with crisis tendencies within the metropole.

Equally important, neoliberalism is more than a matter of economic policy. Jesook Song (2006), in a study of Korean neoliberalism's effacement of homeless women, puts it well by remarking that neoliberalism is a 'sociocultural logic', a social ethos operating through a wide variety of social agents, as well as an economic program. I would put it even more strongly. The neoliberal project is ontoformative, it creates new social realities on a very wide front.

Thus the internal culture of organizations is changed by regimes of individualized 'performance management', by 're-engineering' of business processes. Every medium of communication, from the Internet to the classroom, is invaded by commercial marketing messages. Social movements are transformed into NGOs competing for corporate or state funding. Universities are increasingly dependent on corporate money and models of organization. Even some of the Protestant churches begin to preach the beauty of wealth, in defiance of the gospel.

Family relationships cannot be immune from this powerful project of change. Debates have arisen about the impact of labour market insecurity on 'work/life balance' and about the impact of neoliberal 'welfare reform' on poor families. In this chapter I take these debates as a starting-point to ask the wider question about how neoliberalism is affecting parent–child relationships.

I approach this question by looking at social research about family relationships – specifically, studies conducted in, or shortly after, times of neoliberal transition, when the effects of the neoliberal regime might be thrown into relief. I have focused on four institutional sectors: schooling; family support welfare mechanisms; the workplace/family interface; and the emotional interior of the family. I have sought studies from all continents and from a range of different situations in the global economy. There is a wealth of evidence, limited by the fact that I have been working from English-language reports. In this chapter I focus on two moments in a complex dynamic of change. The first is change in the broad structures of gender and family life, the second is specific change in parent–child relationships.

Reconfiguring gender relations and families

Markets are often presumed to be gender-neutral and the neoliberal agenda should in that case have the effect of eliminating gender inequalities, over time. This is quite compatible with liberal feminism's ideal of a 'level playing field'. Neoliberal managers can and do adopt Equal Employment Opportunity rules and business groups give awards for Businesswoman of the Year to display their commitment to gender equity.

A certain de-gendering of employment has occurred in the last generation. In most of the world's economies there are now few occupations that are absolutely gender-segregated. Even military forces now admit women. But many branches of labour are *mainly* gender-segregated. Aggregate economic inequalities between women and men remain large, even in the most 'developed' countries.

At the top levels and the lead sectors of the neoliberal global economy, there is little gender equality. The number of women in the top management of transnational corporations remains obstinately low: in 2007, 98 per cent of the CEOs of the 500 biggest transnational corporations were men. Trading floors (now increasingly computerized) in international capital markets remain practically a male preserve. Global communication systems are dominated by men and are in many ways hostile to women – the volume of sexist pornography on the Internet is one contemporary index. The international security state apparatus is both managed by men and mainly staffed by men. Whatever 'equal opportunity' exists in principle, the institutional world of neoliberalism is in practice a scene of overwhelming dominance by men.

This may seem like simple reproduction of traditional sex roles. But there is nothing 'traditional' about it. Practically all the institutional system of contemporary global capitalism has been created in the last generation, at most two generations. There is a gender *dynamic* in neoliberalism, a capacity to construct and reconstruct gender orders.

A separation between feminine home and masculine workplace was, as Øystein Holter (1995) argued, usual in the modern European gender order, with many local inflections. One inflection is the Catholic rural tradition described by Harry Ferguson (2001) as dominant in post-independence Eire, where the father/husband's position was marked by hard work, authority and emotional distance. Ferguson argues that the late twentieth-century transformation of postcolonial Ireland into a province of post-industrial Europe has changed this gender order. Softer masculinities, more equal marriages, and more emotionally engaged fatherhood, have become hegemonic.

Similarly in England, in an exceptional three-generation life-history study of fatherhood, Julia Brannen and Ann Nilsen (2006) find a shift from strong gender divisions earlier in the twentieth century, to a hands-on model in the latest generation. They nicely summarize this as a change 'from fatherhood to fathering'. Yet this change is not uniform; some men in the current generation move back towards a work-focused fatherhood, under market pressures. Taga Futoshi traces successive discourses of fatherhood emerging in Japan over the last two generations, with a discourse of fathers as carers now gaining support from the state. The young middle-class Japanese men interviewed by Taga (2001) in the 1990s no longer had the 'salaryman' model of husband/fatherhood as an unquestioned ideal. But they were markedly divided in their ideas about their personal future and the shape of the families they might form. Taga's (2007) recent interviews show Japanese fathers facing conflict and guilt, whatever solution to the problem of work/life balance they attempt.

Similar dynamics are visible in the periphery, perhaps involving sharper conflicts. Mara Viveros Vigoya (2001), reviewing Latin American research on masculinities, suggests that rising expectations of fatherhood become more difficult to meet because of the dislocations caused by neoliberal restructuring. Fatherhood is, in much of Latin America, a key expression of masculinity, but has recently become a site of social conflict and personal difficulty.

There was a trend towards shorter working hours through the nineteenth and twentieth centuries in industrialized economies. Under neoliberalism this trend has been halted and in some places reversed. There is now public discussion of the 'long hours culture' in workplaces and the 'work/life collision' that results (Pocock 2003). As neoliberal regimes have unravelled union and state protection of workers and their conditions, there has been a trend towards longer working days, erosion of leave entitlements and declining security of employment. Research on completely deregulated labour markets, such as Barley and Kunda's (2004) ethnography of 'free agent' computer software contractors in Silicon Valley, shows the open-ended time commitments that result. Heavy demands on time not only flow from the contracted work, but also from the networking, retraining, scanning and negotiating required to survive in such a market.

The advent of neoliberal regimes has created tensions around the emergence of new masculinities. Neoliberal individualism and equal-opportunity ideas promote a diversification of masculinities and a shift towards more equal gender relations. This allows the emergence of a technocratic and mildly libertarian 'transnational business masculinity' in corporate environments (Connell and Wood 2005). At the same time economic insecurity in the deregulated labour market undermines care work by men. Sharpened competition, and very high pay-offs for the successful, in the deregulated corporate world promote a renewal of aggressive, work-focused masculinities in the dominant classes.

The neoliberal agenda has socially divided effects on femininity. 'Welfare reform' in the USA pushed single mothers into the workforce, as did neoliberal measures in other countries (Orloff 2002; Hill 2006). In Nicaragua, following Violeta Chamorro's election in 1990, a neoliberal package was introduced involving public sector cuts, privatization of state agencies and reduced social services. Julie Cupples' (2005) interviews with single mothers in the town of Matagalpa found these changes reflected in mothers' loss of dignity and greater difficulty in making ends meet. But the women of Matagalpa responded actively. With the growth of an informal sector and improvised money-making activities, the women moved into employment, however precarious, more confidently than the men. Having to care for children obliged the women to generate a family income. Over time, Cupples suggests, paid work has become consolidated as part of women's identity, reconciled with maternity rather than opposed to it.

Neoliberalism creates other paths for women into the labour market. Heidi Tinsman's (2000) oral-history research in Chile shows this in the export-oriented fruit industry created under the Pinochet regime – following the core neoliberal strategy of seeking comparative advantage in global markets. Recruited on a large scale for the first time into wage labour, rural women's command of an income, and their ability to make shopping trips and purchasing decisions, changed the balance of power with husbands. Segregated work groups created by employers provided an alternative to domestic isolation and led to new relationships among women. Thus neoliberal restructuring led to a re-shaping of women's work and an erosion of husband's authority that sharply contradicted the dictatorship's official maternalist ideology.

There are, however, limits to this dynamic. Susan Mannon's (2006) study of marriages in the central valley of Costa Rica, with the charming title 'Love in the time of neoliberalism', emphasizes the strength of patriarchal ideology. This, plus the emotional ties between spouses, prevents women from cashing in their new economic strength as a change in marital power. Jill Weigt's (2006) interviews with ex-welfare mothers in the USA show that the insistent official discourse of work enforcement does not necessarily dominate the women's consciousness. It co-exists with an ideology of mothering and another discourse of 'the standard North American family'. All are in play and the women 'navigate' among them. So there has been no gender revolution resulting from women's market participation.

Among privileged classes there has also been a movement into paid work, changing the gender balance in professions such as medicine and public administration and producing those occasional Businesswomen of the Year. But wealth makes this move reversible. In 2003 a New York magazine article about the 'opt-out revolution' sparked a media firestorm about educated upper-middle-class women leaving the workplace in order to be stay-at-home mothers. In this context of economic privilege, as the analysis of US media by Mary Vavrus (2007) shows, the neoliberal rhetoric of context-free 'choice' allows a restoration of traditional images of motherhood.

How many women actually follow this path is not shown by media analysis. Yet the impressive recent growth of the luxury fashion industry, expensive services such as cosmetic surgery, the complex of leisure institutions for rich women, the visibility of trophy wives for rich businessmen and the media's invention of the glamorous but functionless 'celebrity', strongly suggest the growth of a consumption-oriented femininity among the neoliberal rich. There is a tendency, I infer, for neoliberal regimes to generate a class and race polarization of gender patterns. There is a division within femininity between production and consumption orientations, displacing the older polarization on these lines between masculinity and femininity.

How do these shifts in gender relations, and the commodification of social reproduction, affect relationships within families? We know from the sociology of the family that family forms are diverse and subject to change (Gilding 1997). As Harriet Bjerrum Nielsen and Monica Rudberg show in *Psychological Gender and Modernity* (1994), such changes also change the intra-personal dynamics producing gendered subjectivity.

Øystein Holter's (1995) analysis of the hegemonic form of the modern European family helps in understanding the main direction of change. Holter emphasizes not only that the family home is produced as a feminine space in contrast to the masculinity of the outside workplace. Also, the relationships within it are systematically different from those in the capitalist economy. The wife/mother enacts family by managing its 'focal reciprocity', involving gift relationships and emotional connections. It is this emotional base, in Holter's view, that has made family relationships so difficult to change, even in the strong Scandinavian push towards egalitarian, shared-work households.

Yet this pattern of emotional relations is eroded by the expansion of the market, and neoliberal theory shows it. What is Gary Becker's (1981) famous *Treatise on the Family*, if not an extended proof that the bourgeois nuclear family *can* be analysed on a neoliberal market basis and reduced to calculations of individual advantage? Becker's remarkable account of 'superior men' and 'superior women' – in terms of the marriage market – is a *tour de force* of cynicism in which wives and husbands are imagined as entrepreneurs scanning the market and then hiring each other.

If this is not simply a fantasy, but defines a real possibility emergent in neoliberal agendas, we can see neoliberalism as undermining the emotional absolutism of family relations. In psychoanalytic terms, what happens is a de-oedipalization of attachment and desire. For boys, the conditions for the oedipal pattern defined by Freud – fear of paternal authority and desire for the mother – are weakened, if not obliterated. At the same time the conditions for a gender-segregated identification of girls with mothers (Bjerrum Nielsen and Rudberg 1994) are undermined.

Economic effects under neoliberalism *can* lead to more egalitarian and cooperative family practices. A clear example is given by Brannen and Nilsen's (2006) three-generation study in England, in the case of 'Nick', a young father. Nick made a creative response to unemployment including higher involvement with children than the older men in his family. Thrown off welfare in accordance with neoliberal policies, he evolved with his wife a shared strategy combining paid work and parenting for both.

But time-budget studies, which show that men as a group have increased childcare and domestic work very little, strongly suggest that Nick's response is exceptional (Bittman and Pixley 1997). A more common experience is that of Maria Dlamini, the South African contract cleaner at the centre of Bezuidenhout and Fakier's (2006) study of the impact of privatization on public-sector service workers. She and her fellow-workers, their working conditions devastated, responded in a resilient way but got little help with reproductive labour from the men in their communities. Elizabeth Kuznesof (2005) refers to research on the informal urban economy in Brazil that shows an even more drastic departure from the oedipal family. In the community studied, children go out to work, and a group of children may even function as the 'breadwinner' for their mother.

The complex shifts of emotion in neoliberal transition are brilliantly documented in a psychological study of a poor family in Santiago de Chile, by Clara Han (2004). The study focuses on 'Leticia', once a left-wing militant in the Allende period. Forced into exile under the dictatorship, she abandoned her family, which was looked after by her adopted daughter Julieta, who now tries to hold things together economically. Leticia returned and tries, despite her precarious livelihood, to sustain a commitment to *lo social* in the face of post-dictatorship market society. She criticizes other people's political passivity and acceptance of consumerism. Julieta regards her mother as unrealistic, contests her reclaiming of family authority and, though loyal, resents Leticia's careless contracting of debts. Leticia, battling against the tide, suffers what she calls *depresión neoliberal*. Her attempts at restoring everyday life, Han suggests, are continually undermined by neoliberal reality.

Remaking parenthood

Neoliberal transition is likely to disrupt simple transmission of culture from parent to child and thus is likely to reduce the family's role in the overall process of social reproduction. Reasons include the geographical disruption of parent–child relations through labour migration, the disruption of family time by the 'end of welfare' and the long hours culture, as well as the increasing penetration of children's lives by unregulated marketing, commercial mass culture and entertainment media.

A dramatic example of this process is Jakob Rigi's (2003) harrowing ethnography of the consequences of neoliberal shock treatment in Kazakhstan. The minority who won control of economic assets in the great wave of privatizations across the former Soviet republics in the early 1990s were able to insert their children into professional careers or other positions of safety, as well as buying them the goodies of consumer culture – brand-name jeans, electronic equipment and so on. The majority of families were thrown into poverty and insecurity. The parents tended to hold to Soviet-era morality stressing the work ethic and the value of education. The children spurned the old world, reached for consumer culture, but lacked the resources (money or networks) to gain it. The result was a wedge between parents and children and a drift of the youth out of formal education towards apathy, casual work and gendered sources of short-term money such as prostitution, crime and security work. 'Heroic sacrifices' by some working-class parents to support their children's education had little effect.

In Bolivia another disrupting effect becomes clear in Lesley Gill's (2000) ethnography of urban poverty in El Alto. Neoliberal restructuring meant a partial privatization of public [state] schools, including a package of local control. When the drying up of public sector funds produced a teachers' strike, a wedge was inserted between poor parents and the teachers of their children, who became industrial opponents. In Australia, as Deborah Brennan (2002) shows, a state-supported community childcare sector had grown in the 1970s and 1980s, largely on feminist initiative to support mothers in the workforce. Under neoliberalism from the late 1980s on, though state subsidies remained, they were increasingly directed to profit-seeking providers of childcare, and the cooperative centres withered. Thus the corporate sector inserted itself between parents and children on another front. A crisis resulted when the main company concerned, ABC Learning, collapsed in the global financial downturn.

A sense of distance between parent and child is exactly the

problem addressed by the 'new fatherhood', which seeks to restore emotional connection. Sociologists have been understandably sceptical of the 'new father' story, given survey evidence of the glacial pace of change in the gender division of domestic and care work (McMahon 1999). Yet the new fatherhood certainly persists as a cultural ideal, evidence of a problem that many men feel the need to address.

There is evidence from just before the expansion of neoliberalism in Australia that in market-oriented ruling-class schools, fathers played a supervisory and funding role distinct from that of their wives (Connell *et al.* 1982). More recent British research suggests that middle-class parents who are governors and board members of market-oriented schools similarly define their roles in gendered ways, fathers bringing financial expertise, mothers bringing community expertise (Ranson *et al.* 2003).

Neoliberal regimes, rejecting the principle of universal public education, subsidizing private schooling and childcare, and corporatizing public institutions, have created pressures on parents to operate as investors and consumers in a market, competitively maximizing family gains from education. But the market relations investing children are operated through a gender division of labour between parents. Neoliberalism has thus created a 'new fatherhood' of a different kind – the father as manager of the family investment in schooling.

Further, it is private schools, far more than public schools, that maintain gender segregation in education and this is now routinely justified on grounds of parent 'choice'. Gender segregation is now a common theme of marketing for private schools (Mills 2004). A striking consequence of the neoliberal re-shaping of Australian education is the rise of state-funded religious private schools, many of which are segregated and are highly conservative in gender terms. Could we say that neoliberal education thus tends to compensate for the de-oedipalization of the family, by re-oedipalizing the school?

Certainly the neoliberal agenda, as it has moved through other institutional sectors, has found many ways of reinstating gender divisions. Sport is one of the most gender-divided areas of culture in the global metropole. Sport has been increasingly colonized by the market, reconstructed as a commercial competitive enterprise, in ways that maintain sharp gender divisions (Messner 2007). Jay Coakley (2006), a US specialist on youth sport, notes how investing in privatized competitive sport not only allows North American parents to show they are taking individual responsibility for their children's behaviour. It allows them to do this in a gendered way. Through sport, fathers can be active in child-raising as coaches, drivers and team managers, without doing anything to change the gender division of labour in the home.

Neoliberal regimes also have effects on motherhood, also complex. Perhaps the broadest effect of the colonization of reproductive labour by the market is a dis-embodying of motherhood. Less and less of the care and raising of children directly involves the mother's body. The emotion-drenched physical connection in which child development was formerly grounded is thinned out, mediated through institutions and electronic media or confined to a shorter period of life. Yet mothers remain central to reproductive labour, given the slow change in the gender division of labour. In two significant ways motherhood is expanded under neoliberalism.

Henrike Donner's (2006) recent ethnography describing the 'breathtaking' expansion of a private pre-school market in Kolkata finds mothers, specifically, being held accountable for the young child's success in the market world. It is mothers who are under pressure to 'pedagogize' the home – for instance speaking English to the child, buying educational toys, and marginalizing grandparents and servants who speak a local language such as Bengali. In Japan, similarly, there is talk about the 'education mother', who sacrifices a career to focus on the educational advancement of her children – or, perhaps, finds a profession in motherhood. Neoliberalism assigns mothers a moral responsibility for giving their children 'the best possible start in life', for undertaking a planning process in which their children are raised for success in a competitive world. This starts as early as birth. The phrase just quoted comes from a breast-feeding promotion for mothers in Canada (Wall 2001).

The second development concerns mothers who are in the paid

workforce. A recent study of public sector workers in Australia (Connell 2005b) finds women being held responsible for most of the housework and childcare as well as their paid work. Women are also held responsible for *managing the relationship* between household and workplace, that is, for making the work/care regime function. There is every reason to think this is also true in private sector employment. Certainly corporate management takes no responsibility for this issue – it is not even on the radar in business media.

It is not surprising that some mothers in the public sector study describe their lives as spent in 'juggling' all their commitments, and the same word appears in interviews from Barbara Pocock's (2003) study of work/life balance. Nor is it surprising that, because there has been no significant change in the ideology of motherhood (as also in the USA: Weigt 2006), there is widespread guilt among mothers – because the task cannot be done to their own satisfaction.

The note of stress and disillusion, though difficult to pin down, is heard in a number of recent studies of family life under neoliberal regimes. Irina Carlota Silber (2004) records disillusionment in El Salvador after the civil war and the neoliberal settlement, a widespread sense that we are 'worse off than before'. Julie Cupples (2005) traces the loss of dignity among poor people in neoliberal Nicaragua, with demoralization most marked among men, expressed in alcoholism and violence. Rigi's (2003) description of demoralization in the younger generation in neoliberal Kazakhstan has been cited above. In Pocock's (2003) analysis of work/life tension in Australia, the conjuncture of a slow crisis of gender relations with neoliberal labour market deregulation in the 1990s and 2000s has meant stress and fatigue for both men and women. The symptoms of *depresión neoliberal* seem to be widespread.

Conclusions

Let us now consider whether these fragments of evidence form an intelligible pattern. The first conclusion that emerges is that the neoliberal project involves considerable tension between the individualism of market ideology and the social ontoformativity of neoliberal practice, a tension in which patriarchal gender relations are re-shaped but not transcended.

A push towards de-gendering is common in neoliberal institutions, and neoliberal concerns with the rights of the individual and the efficiency of organizations combine to support 'equal opportunity' strategies. Some of the old gender divisions of labour are eroded under this pressure. At the same time, the neoliberal project creates new patriarchal institutions at the heart of the international economy, including transnational management and high-technology industries, and preserves and exploits ideological gender divisions among its subaltern workforces. The project of commodification, as it expands to embrace sports, schooling and other spheres of civil life, reinstates gender division and gender hierarchy in highly divisive ways.

In certain spheres of life, the neoliberal project neither erodes nor reinstates gender division but re-structures gender configurations. The difficulties of doing this among the gender-privileged are apparent in the tensions around the emergence of new masculinities – such as the convinced 'new father' prevented by employment insecurity, economic restructuring or the long-hours workplace from doing care work with his young children. A sharper re-structuring seems to have happened in working-class femininities in neoliberal transitions where motherhood is redefined to include economic provision for the family. A re-structuring of middle-class femininities has also occurred where the task of managing the relationship between home and workplace is added to the social definition of women's work.

I would emphasize that these are not simple or easy changes, but often involve great tension in people's lives as they face conflicting pressures and impossible demands. The prevalence of *depresión neoliberal* may be taken as a measure of the difficulties.

The categories of 'mother' and 'father' are thus caught up in a wider turbulence of change in gender relations. Gender divisions are not becoming obsolete but are, so to speak, turned onto new axes. An important consequence is a certain de-oedipalization of family relationships. The family is less often an arena of unchallenged patriarchy. The embodied and emotional relationships between parents and children are in a number of ways interrupted, mediated or thinned out. Though the stakes of parenthood remain high, the means of action become more limited and the likelihood of direct identification becomes less. Unease about these changes perhaps lies behind the shrill 'family values' rhetoric of many neoliberal regimes.

The neoliberal project, at the same time, creates new means of action for parents, through the market. The commodification of education, especially, re-inserts parents in a realm that had been taken over by the state; but in a new role, that of market agents. For privileged classes, gendered parenthood can now be enacted through the market. Fathers manage families' investments in schooling, while education-mothers provide the informal labour to support their children's passage through commodified pre-school, school, coaching and leisure programmes. In this milieu being a good parent means buying the best services for one's own children.

All this is done under considerable pressure, because such fathers and mothers are also parenting *to* the market. The neoliberal project makes certain features of bourgeois culture obsolete: religiosity, involvement in 'high' culture and social paternalism. What has become obligatory among the privileged is parenting that produces children as effective market agents, able to operate in the environment that the neoliberal project is producing.

Parenting practices oriented to a market world are much more advanced in privileged groups than among the dispossessed, the poor and the less educated. This is starkly shown in the research on families' relationships with neoliberal schooling, where middle-class families embrace the market agenda and working-class families are wedged away from the new mechanisms of educational advantage. Working-class parents are, of course, aware of changing economic realities, but do not have market power to provide commodified education for their children. They often support an expansion of state-based vocational education as the best prospect they can see. This will be explored in Chapter 4.

Motherhood and fatherhood, as social patterns, do not change suddenly; but in time they can change profoundly. In this paper I have assembled evidence that they are changing in the contemporary world under the pressure of the neoliberal project, though not in uniform ways. The changes vary between social classes and between regions of the world and also vary with the differing penetration of neoliberal agendas into social institutions and cultures. We can be sure, nevertheless, that economy and home are now interwoven in new ways, and no understanding of motherhood and fatherhood is now possible without a reckoning with market forces.

4

Working-Class Families and the New Secondary Education

Social class is no longer officially recognized as an issue in Australian life. The working class was often named by political and educational leaders sixty years ago. Now it never appears in policy statements or politicians' speeches, indeed class is rarely mentioned except in vague appeals to a 'middle class' that we are all supposed to belong to. But class is a brute reality in education. Class privilege, class exclusion and other class dynamics shape teaching and learning, across the rich English-speaking countries and far beyond (Bettie 2002; Teese and Polesel 2003).

Throughout the history of public-school systems there have been powerful but ambivalent links with working-class communities. State action to create mass elementary schooling responded to working-class need and desire. Yet the expansion of schooling meant that masses of working-class children and youth spent their time in institutions whose curriculum, pedagogy, assessment and organizational practices were alien to them. As Apple (1993) has argued, the result is cultural subordination, but not simple domination by middle-class ideas.

Both families and schools may change their strategies. Australian schools for instance have attempted multicultural education and introduced compensatory programs with social justice purposes. But reform has always been constrained by privileged social groups seeking to make the education system serve *their* interests. In recent years that desire has been met, above all, by the neoliberal market agenda.

As chapter 3 showed, neoliberalism is a complex movement that operates through a variety of policies. In Australian education there was a squeeze on direct funding of universities, a growth in subsidies to private schools and a strong emphasis on consumer 'choice'. Ideologically, the parents of school children are re-defined as customers rather than citizens. This trend was dramatically confirmed in 2009 with the launch, by a neoliberal Labor Party government, of the 'MySchool' website, publishing test results school by school across the country, immediately followed by 'league tables' constructed by the mass media.

Australian research in the 1970s showed a structural difference between school systems: the ruling class was linked to the system of elite private schools through a market, while the working class was linked to state and Catholic schools through bureaucracies (Connell, Ashenden, Kessler and Dowsett 1982). The neoliberal agenda has, in effect, tried to reconstruct mass education on the model of ruling-class education. Since neoliberal language does not acknowledge that class exists, this is never explicitly acknowledged. It is simply assumed that the market model is universally applicable.

British research shows that this is far from true. The market agenda tends to divide state schools. Schools able to establish links with a middle-class clientele can embrace the market agenda, act entrepreneurially to attract more pupils from whom good exam results can be expected, and tend to shed hard-to-teach groups of pupils. Schools without such clienteles are liable to become residualized, attracting only a local clientele, 'losing' in exam and test competition, and therefore losing in the competition for enrolments and funds. It is not surprising that working-class parents are at best ambivalent about the idea of 'school choice'; the system is structured to produce failure for their children, in new forms (Reay 2001).

This chapter explores the relationship between working-class families and schools in a system influenced by neoliberalism, but also trying to implement social justice reforms.

The study

In the late 1990s the public-school system in New South Wales (NSW) began a reform of upper-secondary curriculum and certification. The reform was supposed to increase both equity and rigour. As part of the equity agenda, vocational or technical courses (known as VET) were to be included in the university selection process, hoping to make that process more socially inclusive. This dovetailed with a national reform of technical education that had produced a new qualifications framework, and school courses were re-designed to fit this framework. It was hoped that these changes would make the schools more attractive to working-class youth and thus encourage retention in school. A growth of VET enrolments did in fact occur.

In 2000–3 these reforms were studied in a project undertaken by staff of the University of Sydney, the Department of Education and Training and the NSW Board of Studies. The study involved close-focus research in eight secondary schools across NSW, chosen to reflect the social and geographical diversity of the public education system.

This chapter draws on information from four schools. Three are classified by system statistics as 'low SES' and one as 'medium SES'. Two are urban and two rural. Their catchments include some of the most recent and poorest immigrant groups in Australia and also the oldest and most economically disadvantaged community. The occupations of parents were very diverse, including housewife, welder, bus driver, school assistant, clerk, small farmer, motel owner/operator, pensioner, clothing outworker and truck driver. This seems characteristic of the contemporary Australian working class, with the decline of large-scale industrial employment and the rise of service industries, temporary and part-time employment and small-scale entrepreneurship.

Interviews were conducted with students in Year 11 and 12 VET classes, their teachers, as many of their parents as could be reached, and other school staff: a total of approximately forty interviews per school. Site visits were made over a period of two years. VET classes and school events were visited by the project team. Focused interviews were undertaken with parents, following a common agenda of topics but with full flexibility in detail. All were conducted by members of the project staff, tape-recorded and later transcribed.

The transcripts were indexed and case studies were written with constant reference to the full text of the interviews. Confidential case studies were written both for individual families and for each school and its community. Case studies were workshopped by the project team, to subject all interpretations to critical scrutiny. This chapter is based on four school case studies, ten family case studies and further analysis covering all students interviewed in the four schools.

Family projects

Markets work only to the extent that people operate them. Markets therefore have to intersect with projects, that is, coherent and persisting patterns of action which link the present with some imagined future. Parents hope their children will pick up the idea. Robyn, a student at Korana High, has certainly done so:

> (How much influence do you think your parents have had?) A lot. (Do you think that's good?) Yep. Because if they weren't behind me, I'd be a bum and drop out of school in Year 10. (Really, why?) I don't want to be known as someone who dropped out of school. Knowing that I could have had more, if I had of stayed at school and finished Year 12.

The family project may concern education without seeking meritocratic advancement through education. It may instead centre on making prudent or appropriate choices. Yasmine, for instance, describes extended discussions about a trade for her son Malik, at Brighton High:

> Basically to us he said 'I like wood.' You know, he likes to do stuff with wood and that. I spoke to one of his teachers once, she goes, 'Your son doesn't like to sit in an office, you know. If you're going to choose a job for him, don't make him sit in an office because he doesn't like to be cramped in' . . . By the time he finished Year 10, I said to him, his Dad kept asking him, 'you still interested in construction and stuff like that?' He goes 'Yeah'. We started looking and that, we didn't push him, but. He was a bit undecided at the beginning, Should I leave school, shall I do that? You know. It was too confusing.

Malik in fact left school in Year 11 to start a carpentry apprenticeship.

Not all family projects centre on education. Maritza is the fourth of six children and she goes to the same school as Malik. Her father is a welder, retired with back injuries after thirty years of factory work, her mother a full-time houseworker. The parents have networks in the Lebanese immigrant community, but their life centres in the family. They support Maritza's education, believe it is important for their children to get the Higher School Certificate (HSC). But they have no particular strategy for her and they rely on Maritza and the school to make the right decisions about education.

It is a mistake to think that concern with education, or interest in education, is lacking in working-class families. But there are certainly class differences in the know-how with which parents approach schooling issues and in the definition of the main problem they have to address. Engaged middle-class parents are likely to be focused on what post-school pathways their children will be launched into. This concern makes strategic choice of subjects, and maximizing marks, the centre of attention. Engaged working-class parents are more likely to be focused on keeping their children in school to get the basic qualification, which currently means the HSC. This concern makes interest and discipline the centre of attention.

For instance Wynona, who regretted her own abandoned education ('I blew my chance at school'), fought to keep her son Mike going to school after finishing the School Certificate. She lost:

> He was just sitting around bludging and he didn't want to get up. I'd just slap him around the head and 'Get on with it!' And it drove me to nearly a nervous breakdown. Cause you've got a husband on your back, 'Get him out and get a job!' And then you've got him, won't get moving. So, it was tough times. But he's turned out not a bad kid.

To everyone's astonishment, Mike brought himself back to school, after a traumatic period in the workforce. He is now doing well at Korana High, despite poverty and family breakdown in his immediate environment.

Parent/child negotiations around schooling

In some of the families we interviewed, the parents were actively involved in schooling decisions. They would read the literature that the school sent home and talk through choices with the children. They would be likely to monitor homework and might coach the students in particular subjects (or arrange for someone else to provide coaching). Some would gather information about TAFE (Technical and Further Education) courses, arrange an apprenticeship, talk with other parents or with teachers.

For immigrant communities, the obvious difficulties are language and lack of familiarity with specifics of the Australian education system. Anglo parents as well as immigrant parents may find their capacity to help their children is limited because the high school curriculum has changed, or because the children are now studying at a level beyond the parents' knowledge. This was most often mentioned in relation to Mathematics. But the same situation had now arisen with English, where the new curricula puzzle or annoy some of the parents.

There is another constraint on parents' involvement in educational decisions – the children. Students in Years 11 or 12, aged fifteen to eighteen, are typically engaged in establishing independence from their parents. Many of them keep their parents short of information about all aspects of their lives, as part of the process of establishing autonomy. So the ebullient Shauna struggles to learn how her daughter Pam is getting on at Korana High:

> No. I've got to drag it out of her [laughs]. She sort of – mainly keeps everything inside herself. She doesn't express herself. She's not like me . . . (Did you come along to any parent information nights for Year 11 and 12?) No, not really. When I did know about them, it was too late. I don't know what it is with Pam. She sort of either forgets to tell me or, I find . . . the information sheets in her room and think 'Oh!' . . . So, no, I hadn't really been to any . . . I confronted her about it. 'Oh, sorry Mum. I forgot.'

There is nothing malicious about this, it is just a very common and quite effective means for a teenager to establish autonomy. And parents may be wary of pushing too hard. Robyn, for instance, the girl who remarks she would 'be a bum' if it weren't for her parents' support, discussed courses with her father, Simon. He pointed her towards commerce and also insisted that she do Maths in Year 11. But he is cautious about pushing this choice because he does not want to get into a fight that will upset her exam preparation. And if she digs her heels in, he will cut his losses:

> You can only do so much with sixteen year olds . . . With the younger kids, they give you more control and you can do a little bit more forcing. But with Robyn, if she turned around and said to me 'I'm not doing Maths next year', I couldn't do anything about it. All I can do is speak to her in a logical manner and tell her all the pros and cons about her not doing Mathematics – and make her own decision.

The commonest solution to this problem, so common that it is the modal pattern of parent/child interaction among our respondents, is for the parents to discuss subject choice with their children, but then let the children make the final choice. In this process the students' interest in the subject is the major criterion, interwoven with ideas about possible jobs, information from older siblings and friends, and experience with similar courses up to Year 10.

We encountered some families where the parents' involvement had dropped to a minimal level. In one case a mother had made a conscious decision that there was little she could do and that study was essentially the child's domain. In another case the mother, Ghada, found it very difficult to get relevant information:

> When I was in Lebanon, I ask a neighbour or someone I know, if I don't understand a question. But here, nobody to ask.

Neither parent in this family knew much about the curriculum at Brighton High. Both found it difficult to help children with their homework because their English is not fluent enough. They provide a computer but feel they cannot help much more. Given that our research almost certainly over-sampled families with close connections to the schools, it is probable that the pattern of distance seen in Ghada's family is also a common one in working-class communities.

For many parents simply keeping the kids at school is the key issue. Sabrina, a mother at Korana High, is doing this in the light of history. She hated school herself, left at fifteen and in those days was able to walk into a job. She knows you cannot do that any more, with downsizing everywhere and the risk of unemployment. Her own husband, a skilled tradesman, has twice been thrown out of work. So she is determined her four children will go right through school and get the HSC. She is adamant about this. She runs a tight ship to make sure it happens with her son Harry:

> He didn't want to go and do Year 11 and 12 at all, but I told him that the same rules apply to him as what applied to the other three. He didn't have a choice in it and if he wanted to renege he had too much to lose. Even now he sometimes says 'I'm not going to school tomorrow' and I say, 'Yeah right, in your dreams! You're going. You've got

too much to lose. You want your car taken off you? Do you want your motor bike taken off you?' And that's it.

No nonsense about freedom of choice, or youth out of control, here! But this Iron Lady strategy is not one that most parents could bring off, even if they wanted to.

Families' interactions with schools

At one end are the positively engaged parents, like Sabrina. At the other extreme are the families who hardly show up on the school's radar at all. One such parent is Susan, a member of an ethnic minority that is the target of some local prejudice. Susan is highly interested in education, having once been a primary school teacher herself, in another country. She was active in relation to her daughter's primary schooling. But she is intimidated by the high school, fears the teachers will be prejudiced against her as an Asian or will not understand her accent. And though she would like to go to parent/teacher nights, she does not, because she cannot drive and is 'scared to go in the evening'. She is a small woman and her fear of walking alone at night through the streets of a rough neighbourhood is reasonable.

There are also parents who are involved, but not happily. Some parents described unsympathetic treatment by the system or school staff. A pattern of conflict can develop where the family defines the school, or particular teachers, as unjust, insensitive or abusive, while the school defines the parent or the child as a trouble-maker or a liar. Parents come to the school, not to help with work, but to contest decisions about the child (unfair marking, disciplinary decisions, etc.). The family considers itself to be 'standing up for its rights', may see the trouble as a class put-down and in that case will draw on the tradition of working-class resistance to authority.

Consider, for instance, the nuances of this story, told by an angry mother. Thora detailed a series of problems with Korana

High and other schools, where she had protested over difficulties such as erratic marking, and went on:

> That was another thing, Matthew's band at the school this year. You know the Rock Eisteddfod band challenge. They've been playing for this band since he was in Year 8, they've been playing for this school, right? At all assemblies, they are very proud of this band. Yet when he asked the teacher if they were being entered into the Rock thing this year, 'No, you're not good enough for that. You don't want to embarrass the school.' How rude! Do you know what they did to my son? – Boom. But do you know what they also did, back up there? He came straight back, because he came home to me and I said 'Don't you take that sitting down. Fancy them telling you that. You've been playing for every assembly and Open Day.' So he did. Came back up here. I don't believe it ever went in [the Eisteddfod], but it was filmed in the hall, they did film it. Only because Matthew and the band kicked up a stink and said 'How dare you say we're not good enough! Give us a go!'

Both sides have a lot to lose in such conflicts. The school stands to lose credibility, community respect, staff time and possibly students. The family loses time, energy and the benefits of goodwill from teachers.

Between these groups is the modal position: parents who may come to parent information nights and discussions of their children's report cards, and who will come to the school when a specific problem arises, but will not come much more than that. This can be a question of practicability. Asked if Junction High did anything to help boys with literacy, Claire answered:

> Well, not that I'm aware of. But that wouldn't mean that I would [know] – because, though I've got three representatives at this school, I never get a school newsletter. I could go to the P & C meetings. But I was involved in the [Primary School] P & C very heavily and so I couldn't do everything. I had to be home some time, so my children could look at me.

But it can also be a question of the parent's capacity to help. Zoe of Korana High, asked if she was happy with the information about subject choice given by the school, answered:

> Yeah, I was. But I think that they should be sat down and talked to more about it. Not just given a couple of papers and, you know, going home with it . . . Like me, I didn't become anything when I was [at school]. So how would I know how to tell Grant what to go for, what your needs are and that? And George [her husband], he never – I suppose he was always slow at school, he never excelled at anything, schoolwise. So how would he know to sit down with Grant and tell Grant where? . . . Grant's got twice the brain we've got. And Norm. I do think it's up to mainly school.

There is also a darker side to the school/family interaction, even for well-run schools in generally supportive communities. The Principal of Rivertown High, for instance, notes episodes where teachers have been threatened by angry parents. Like others in the study this school has been affected by vandalism. Under HSC rules the schools are required to monitor attendance and issue warnings where attendance is inadequate; and the Youth Allowance is affected by school enrolment. Family poverty makes this a tougher issue, as in the communities served by these four schools the Youth Allowance may be a significant part of household income.

Families' reliance on schools for guidance, schools' limited channels of communication to families, and pupils' need for autonomy, result in a potentially damaging paradox about the selection of subjects. As the education system multiplies 'choices' and the consequences of choosing become ever more important, actual responsibility for making the decisions falls mainly on the pupils. They are the group who have least knowledge of the wider world, and they are making choices with guidance that is (in the judgement of many teachers) not very effective. 'They're giving them sweet stuff-all advice', says one teacher, and another at the same school more temperately remarks that many who start Year 11 'don't have any idea of what they want to do or what subject they want to be in, despite all of the guidance and advice'.

Choice and the market

The main educational choice explored in our interviews is choice of subjects for Year 11 and 12, especially the choice of VET subjects. This is a kind of choice that is highly meaningful to our participants. The bases of choice are interest in the subject and success with related subjects in the past; relevance to a working life in the future; and availability, governed by school offerings and timetable constraints. None of the working-class parents mentions an attempt to position their children for higher education.

How are the choices made? The students read the booklet given them by the school, describing the available courses. Some families go to an information night (where the Board of Studies' message to give priority to students' interest in the subject is faithfully communicated). The students often talk it over with parents and other family members and doubtless with friends. They then juggle with the timetable to see how many of their preferred courses they can fit in. The school apparently emphasizes that the ultimate choice is the students'. In practice the students not only have the ultimate responsibility but seem to have the main carriage of the whole process.

That concerns choice of subjects within a school. 'School choice' in the sense of the neoliberal agenda, that is consumer-style choice between schools, is a different matter. The parents have carriage of this issue.

Many are not responding to market structures at all. In about half of the families we interviewed, the parents had not considered anything but a public school and most had automatically gone to the local public school. For some parents this was a taken-for-granted matter. It was how the parents' schooling was organized and it is how the kids' schooling is organized too. For other parents, sending their children to the local public school involved a positive commitment to comprehensive or inclusive education.

Some parents had a commitment to a specific school. In a country town like Rivertown, the centre of a fairly stable though economically depressed rural area, whole families might have gone to the same school for two or three generations. Even in the city, a family may develop strong ties to a local school as several children go there in turn. Sometimes parents knew of an alternative and did not like it. Holly, a parent at the rural Junction High, distrusted a nearby 'senior college' because it gave the kids too much freedom:

> Alesha has had some friends that have left here and gone [to senior college]. But I don't think it ever really works out for them. Here at least they're at school. They're not walking up and down the streets and they're doing their subjects . . . Some perhaps can't get the subjects they want here. But I don't know. We've always been satisfied with it anyway.

Other families, however, do respond to educational markets. The decisions were sometimes explained in considerable detail. Zoe and her husband, for instance, have kept Norm at Korana High but have sent Grant to a Catholic school. This family is not well off. Zoe is Catholic, which helps explain the decision about Grant. But this choice is not primarily about religion. Grant is seen in the family as the one with intelligence, 'he just had a brain about him' and might become a lawyer. Giving him the best shot at this means sending him to a school with discipline, 'because I knew the stricter they are, the better they are'. This involves several negative comparisons with Korana High. 'I don't want him getting comments' – there is a stigma attached to Korana. 'Every girl wants him' – he will be distracted by sex, but the Catholic school is segregated. 'All the boys hate him' – studious and popular with the girls, he gets bullied. 'Too many Islanders . . . Filipinos. I don't like putting him somewhere where one race dominates.'

Such decisions, which other working-class families besides Zoe's had made or considered, did not generally have the character of a consumer maximizing utilities in a market. Rather, these decisions generally had a *defensive* character. They concerned a child perceived as in some way vulnerable, where the local state school offers a threat from which the parent wished to protect the child. The threat may be one of disorder and violence, or disliked ethnic groups (Aborigines and Pacific Islanders are repeatedly mentioned by white parents), or a peer culture opposed to learning. 'White flight' has not generally been thought an issue in Australian education. But on the evidence of this set of interviews, it is an issue of significance for the public-school system. School choice probably speeds up processes of ethnic concentration and segregation for other reasons too, such as families from a particular immigrant group bringing their children together for mutual support.

Conclusion

Vocational education was, historically, the bearer of a specific kind of class consciousness, centred on male-dominated manual trades and expressed in their occupational cultures (Mealyea 1993). In the high schools we studied there is still something of this flavour around VET teaching. There is a pride in trade skills, a marked scepticism of authority, an informality and an egalitarian social outlook.

A kind of oppositional class consciousness is also found among some of the parents whose children are doing vocational courses. Sabrina for instance is proud of her neighbourhood, angry with people who put it down, proud of her family's practical skills, critical of academic arrogance and corporate greed: 'they have given themselves great big pay rises . . . and working people down the bottom are suffering'. She is also fearful for her children, in a future of greater insecurity.

But there is now, in Australian working-class life, no collective way of responding to this. The unions are weak and defensive, the Australian Labor Party has gone neoliberal, the popular media are commercial and increasingly right-wing. Sabrina and parents like her are left with the defensive strategy of trying to ensure the employability of their individual children. That fuels their support for VET. It may also fuel ethnic divisiveness (not in Sabrina's outlook, but certainly in others) and conservative views of the content and method of education. All this makes it difficult for schools serving working-class communities to explore new pedagogies.

The system's efforts in expanding vocational education are paying off in terms of goodwill, but the overall impact is still limited. Most families expect only minor occupational benefits from VET courses. In this, they share the opinion of many of the VET teachers themselves.

The market agenda, in an explicit and developed form, is not prominent in these families' relationship with education. It is of course a powerful background presence, limiting investment in public schools and making the 'choice' of private schooling cheaper, through subsidies. But the working-class families we interviewed are not market-oriented, they do not generally see themselves as utility-maximizers. In this sense our findings are subtly different from the 'ambivalence' reported in Britain by Reay and Ball (1997). Here, there is a certain *absence* from the market or from market-type behaviour.

Rather than trying to maximize individual gains, the educational project these working-class families most often had was getting their children to the new minimum, the HSC. They still heavily depend, as working-class families did a generation ago, on the bureaucratic machinery of state education to deliver a reasonable education for their children.

There is still a great deal of goodwill and respect for schooling and some schools make very good use of it. But one cannot say that the educational experience of working-class families in general is supportive and productive. In the 1970s and early 1980s an agenda of democratic reform in Australian schools was moving in that direction. In the later 1980s and 1990s neoliberalism derailed it and substituted a market agenda. The very mixed picture we see now is the consequence.

5

Good Teachers on Dangerous Ground

Anyone concerned with the quality of education or concerned with social justice in education – and I think the two issues are very closely linked – must be concerned with teachers. However well a curriculum is designed, however well a school system is planned, it is teachers who have to make it work, day by day, in the classroom and playground. It is teachers who have to deal with the diversity of students and the effects of social inequalities in students' lives and learning. Teachers are the workforce of reform.

Teachers make a specific kind of workforce. What they do in schools is never just conveying a set of facts to pupils. Teachers necessarily *interpret* the world for, and with, their pupils. This is obvious in early childhood education. But it is equally true in the most technical subjects in high school, where interpretation is embedded in the language, selection of objects of knowledge and mental operations of a given subject area.

Interpreting the world for others, and doing it well, requires not just a skill set but also a knowledge of how interpretation is done, the cultural field in which it is done and the other possibilities of interpretation that surround one's own. Teaching is, inherently, intellectual labour and teachers are a group of intellectual workers.

Not just 'knowledge workers' in a knowledge economy, but specifically *intellectual* workers (see chapter 6). Teachers in their daily
work operate with forms of understanding as well as bodies of facts,
and necessarily transform the culture as they convey it to the next
generation.

As neoliberal agendas have moved into education systems, they
have developed an interest in teachers. In 2002 the Organization
for Economic Cooperation and Development, the economic think
tank for the rich countries, launched a big project on 'teacher
policy' which eventually drew in 25 countries. Three years later
the report was published, announcing with an air of discovery that
'teachers matter' (OECD 2005). In Australia, all states and territo-
ries have recently become concerned with teacher accountability
(Kleinhenz and Ingvarson 2004). Even the Business Council, a
capitalist peak body not normally suspected of concern for the
public interest, has come out with a report on teacher quality
called *Teaching Talent*, arguing for higher pay for high-performing
teachers (Business Council of Australia 2008).

A concern with teacher quality might suggest that governments
wanting to improve education would be pouring vast resources
into teacher education. That hasn't happened. What *has* happened
is that governments in the rich countries are building an imposing
new apparatus of testing, accreditation and surveillance. A new
front seems to have opened in the old struggle to control teachers' labour. In this chapter I want to explore these developments,
taking the Australian case where the machinery is already well
developed and thinking about the wider implications for education
and social justice.

The changing idea of the good teacher

It is clear that ideas of what makes a good teacher have shifted
historically. When public-school systems were being created by
colonial governments in Australia, pupil–teacher schemes and
training schools aimed at the narrow set of pedagogical skills

required for a tightly controlled school curriculum. But they also had a strong moral agenda emphasizing respectability and obedience (Hyams 1979).

As the need to staff a secondary school system developed, a greater intellectual content was required. In the early twentieth century Teachers' Colleges claimed a little independence and brought a whiff of New Education and the American psychology of learning into Australian teacher training. A strong emphasis on social conformity and rule-following remained. For instance, in *The Groundwork of Teaching* (Mackie 1924), the textbook written by staff of the Sydney Teachers' College, there was no questioning of the State as the sole source of authority. Students were given a great deal of hard-headed advice on everyday life in schools, lesson plans, tests and administrative procedures. Yet *The Groundwork* also had an essay on 'The Vocation of the Teacher', written by a classics master, which emphasized the need for imagination and drama in teaching and advised teachers not to stick too closely to the textbook.

As Sandra Acker (1983) observed in Britain, there was a strong tendency to see women teachers in terms of family roles. For women, the idea of a good teacher was liable to be blurred with the idea of a good mother. For men, an ideology of professionalism made better sense. A technical model of teaching was encouraged by the spread of intelligence and achievement testing between the wars. This was linked with an ideology of educational hierarchy, of natural differences in intelligence or educability, that had socially conservative overtones. It sat awkwardly with educational reform in the following generation, which saw a surge in working-class demand for education, the rapid growth of comprehensive high schools from the 1950s to the 1970s, moves towards gender equality and the opening of universities and colleges.

Therefore the technical-professional model did not carry all before it. Teacher education was gradually moving into universities, and universities in the mid twentieth century were still a site of humanistic learning. This yielded an idea of the good teacher who not only knew how to run a classroom but also had learned how to think for herself, apply disciplined knowledge and act as an agent of cultural renewal. The quality of teaching and the purposes of democracy were linked by a kind of mass humanism, embedded in common-learnings curricula and translated by a workforce of intellectually autonomous, university-educated teachers. A scholar–teacher ideal was articulated in the most widely circulated postwar teacher education textbook, *The Foundations of Education*, produced by staff at the University of Sydney (Connell *et al.* 1962).

In other hands, the combination of humanist ideas and teaching skills generated the 'reflective practitioner' model and initiatives for school-level democracy and teacher-developed curricula, which became powerful in the 1970s. This trend in Australia broadly corresponded with the ideas of 'critical pedagogy' and 'teachers as intellectuals' developed in North America about the same time (Giroux 1988).

This model was vulnerable in several ways. In the fields of knowledge considered foundational to education, powerful critiques of disciplinary knowledge (such as postmodernist deconstruction) emerged internationally. At the same time, changes in the schools' social environment undermined general education. Youth unemployment rose in the 1970s and remained obstinately high, challenging the belief that schooling could be trusted to deliver economic security. There was always a whiff of the missionary about the humanist agenda. Humanist learning was never easy to translate into a coherent programme for working-class children – who remained the majority of participants in public schools.

In contemporary Australian education, though there are still differing ideas of what makes a good teacher, one holds the dominant position. I call this the 'competent teacher' model because it centres on an assemblage of competencies attributed to good teachers. It is much the same idea of the teacher that Alex Moore (2004) in England calls the 'competent craftsperson' and Everard Weber (2007) in South Africa more critically calls the 'compliant technician'.

In the restructuring of technical and further education (TAFE) since the 1980s, distinct skills or competencies were extracted from the matrix of traditional apprenticeships, packaged and taught as separate modules. Specific, measurable outcomes, rather than broad trade-based identities, became the goal of vocational education. The teacher-competency model followed this approach and thus connected with the growth of a market-oriented political and cultural order, discussed in other chapters of this book, especially managerialism and the development of 'audit culture' (Power 1997).

Two developments in the education sector gave a sharp edge to these changes. The first was the growing attention by policymakers to multivariate quantitative research on school and teacher 'effectiveness'. This research treats schools and teachers as bearers of variables (attitudes, qualifications, strong leadership, etc.) to be correlated with pupil outcomes, measured on standardized tests. This gave an educational interpretation to the managerialist idea – derived from the muddled discourse of 'excellence' in corporate management – that there is always a 'best practice' that can be instituted and audited from above.

The second was neoliberal governance of teaching itself. This is different from the professional form of control-at-a-distance. Market-oriented neoliberalism is profoundly suspicious of professionalism; it regards professions as anti-competitive monopolies. Specifically, neoliberalism distrusts teachers. This has gone further in some countries than others, as Doherty and McMahon (2007) observe in a comparison of Scotland with England; but the trend is general.

Under a neoliberal regime, educational institutions must *make themselves auditable*. The audit culture in education has included the push for national testing, for 'league tables' of schools considered as firms competing with each other, and for the creation of teacher registration institutions which are deliberately separated from teacher education institutions. The lists of competencies for teachers these institutions produce are also lists of auditable performances.

The consequences for teacher education are potentially very large. A list of auditable competencies can become the whole rationale of a teacher education programme. There is no need, in such a model, for any conception of Education as an intellectual discipline. There is no need for cultural critique, since the market, aggregating individual choices, decides what services are wanted and what are not. There is a limited role for educational research, mainly to do positivist studies to discover 'best practice'.

There is still a need to teach specific curriculum areas, so subject-specific knowledge and skills are needed. Technical skills, including competence in new technologies, are required. Those are the main services that schools offer to the market and there will be a continuing demand for them. But there is no need for the competent teacher to be able to reflect on the bodies of knowledge from which the school curriculum derives. That is the business of the central authorities, which audit the outcomes of the schools' work. Teacher-generated curriculum becomes an absurdity, because it cannot be competitively assessed. In short, under the new regime of educational governance, the humanist model of the good teacher becomes an anachronism. What, exactly, replaces it? The teacher registration bodies themselves have an answer.

How the good teacher is defined in the new registration regime

The most important definitions of the good teacher current in Australian education are the Standards documents of the new registration bodies. These follow a common format, though they have many variations in detail. The Standards documents consist of lists of sentences or clauses which state something that teachers do or should do. For instance:

Develop a calm and approachable demeanour. (Tasmania: graduate level, B.3 indicator 4)

Teachers are familiar with curriculum statements, policies, materials and programs associated with the content they teach. (Victoria: full registration level, col. 2 no. 4)

Initiate or lead the implementation of policies and processes to integrate ICT into the learning environment. (NSW: professional leadership level, no. 1.4.4)

The terser documents have about thirty such statements, the more expansive about 130, at each of four career levels. The statements are classified under broad headings such as 'Professional Knowledge', 'Professional Practice' and 'Professional Engagement'; these headings vary slightly from state to state, but have much in common.

The substantive sentences have no connection with each other. They are simply dot points. You could go on adding more dot points – as some state committees obviously have – or you could subtract them, without affecting the framework. The lists do not come from any systematic view of Education as a field of knowledge.

Parallel lists of statements are offered at each of four levels, from just-graduated to 'leadership'. The statements at the top levels are on the whole vaguer than those at the lower levels. Nevertheless, the idea that teachers can be sorted into a hierarchy of professional levels is a major formal component of the notion of standards made operational by the Institutes. The stratification of the workforce that is sought by neoliberal agendas of individual competition among workers is thus built into the definition of teacher professionalism.

In content, the lists are hybrid. They include summaries of educational literature, subject-specific knowledges, generalized educational approaches, specific pieces of know-how needed to operate in a school, and statements of attitudes or beliefs that teachers should hold. Some statements are hybrid within themselves. From the Victorian Institute of Teaching's (2008) *Standards for Graduating Teachers*, the statement 'Be aware of how curriculum and assessment is structured to support learning' suggests a piece of organizational know-how. But it also embeds an attitude, that is, accepting that curriculum and assessment *are* structured to support learning. Would a student teacher who concluded that the current system of assessment actively *interferes with* learning (as it probably does, for at least half the students in our schools), meet the professional standard? I would hope so, but the Standards documents do not encourage me to believe so. The cautions, admonitions and invitations to conformity heavily outnumber the invitations to take wing.

In this respect the Standards documents are very traditional. They contain the mixture of background knowledge, pedagogical skills, organizational know-how, ideology and social conformity that has always been expected of the workforce of a mass school system, since the nineteenth century.

They are hybrid because school teaching itself involves a hybrid labour process. As every close-focus study of school life shows, teaching's daily reality is an improvised assemblage of a very wide range of activities (Connell 1985). The fact that different state committees, made up of experienced teachers and administrators, came up with different dot-point lists, *which sound equally convincing*, is itself a very good indication of the improvised multiplicity of practices involved in teaching.

In other respects, however, the Standards documents reveal something new. Their language is strongly influenced by corporate managerialism. The texts are heavy with 'challenges', 'goals', 'stakeholders', 'partnerships', 'strategies', 'commitment', 'capacity', 'achievable', 'effective', 'flexible' and 'opportunities'.

These terms have a powerful rhetorical effect. They construct the good teacher as an entrepreneurial self, forging a path of personal advancement through the formless landscape of market society with its shadowy stakeholders and its endless challenges and opportunities.

The Standards statements include a lot of the organizational common-sense of school teaching and teacher education. They have been welcomed by some as a public definition of professionalism that displays the complex work that teachers do and the difficulty of doing it well. Given how fiercely teachers in public schools have been abused by the political Right over the last thirty years, this is helpful. The Standards may also help protect education against abuses of the 'charismatic' image of the good teacher, where politicians in search of publicity throw untrained youngsters into very difficult teaching situations on the Hollywood principle that natural talent will triumph in the last reel.

But such benefits come at a price. The Standards framework embeds the neoliberal distrust of teachers' judgement. What teachers do is decomposed into specific, auditable competencies and

performances. The framework is not only specified in managerialist language. It embeds an individualized model of the teacher
that is deeply problematic for a public education system, and a
top-down approach to control. It is not surprising that in the 2010
national election, the neoliberal Labor Party prime minister, Julia
Gillard, announced as her main education policy a competitive
system of rewards for high-achieving schools and teachers – the
policy advocated by the Business Council – a proposal promptly
matched by the opposition leader. No consultation with teachers
occurred.

Towards a new understanding of good teachers

The divisiveness of the neoliberal agenda is clear and many experienced educators are deeply unhappy with it. But there is not yet
a substantial alternative to offer. One step has to be developing a
better conception of 'good teachers'. In this section I offer ideas on
four key issues that have emerged in recent research and debate:
the work of teaching, teaching as an occupation, the intellectual
structure of education, and educational process.

Teachers' work. Teaching is a form of labour, undertaken in
specific workplaces, in certain employment relations. Teacher
education *is* the making of a workforce. As Alan Reid (2003)
argues, we need an analysis of this labour process in education, if
we are to get beyond the micro focus of most recent research on
teaching.

The Standards statements do recognize this dimension of teaching, when they refer to the capacities needed to operate in a school
environment. But they only acknowledge the labour process in
a limited way and we need to broaden the vision. For instance,
school teaching is *embodied* labour, in which the physical presence
of the teacher in interaction with the student is important (Estola
and Elbaz-Luwisch 2003). Energy, movement, expression and
fatigue all matter. In one of the most striking studies ever done
about teacher quality, Gerald Grace (1978) interviewed teachers in

London inner-city schools nominated by their principals as 'good teachers'. He found that they were steadily burning themselves out, becoming exhausted trying to respond to the endless demands of total involvement. What is the use of any model of the good teacher where the good teachers self-destruct? Good teaching must be *sustainable*; and that can only be planned when we see teaching as a practicable labour process.

Further, teaching involves a great deal of emotion work (Hebson *et al.* 2007; Connell 1985). Classroom life involves a flow of emotions, both on the part of the teachers and the pupils, ranging from simple likes and dislikes to enthusiasm, anxiety, boredom, joy, fear and hope. All teachers have to manage this flow and make it productive for the pupils' learning and survivable for themselves. Learning to do this is a large part of the proverbial 'first year out', the early stage of a teaching career.

The emotional aspect of teachers' labour process can be included in competency models – the Standards documents just discussed have occasional statements like 'Develop a calm and approachable demeanour'. But such dimensions are extremely difficult to assess and under pressure are likely to be sidelined by other issues, especially test performance. A frightening recent study of 'capability' proceedings in English schools shows that this actually happens (Hebson *et al.* 2007). A study of restructuring in the same country (Stevenson 2007) showed a re-alignment of teaching focused on what management regarded as the core task of teaching, that is, the technical part. This downplayed the 'pastoral' functions. This may improve a school's competitive position in the league tables. It is difficult to believe it results in better education for the children.

Neoliberal personnel management defines the worker as an entrepreneurial individual and tries to eliminate the collective agency of workers expressed through unions (Compton and Weiner 2008). How much the labour process of teaching has changed recently under neoliberal pressure is open to debate. What is clear, however, is the agenda of individualization. Institutionally, the Standards documents define the object of registration and evaluation as an individual teacher.

Yet even the single-teacher classroom is part of a complex institution, the school, and the teacher is part of a local workforce. School and staff are parts of larger institutional systems and workforces. The familiar 'outcomes' of education are strongly defined by this structured environment, including the very measures of student performance used to assess individual teachers. Standardized tests of educational achievement are, to a striking degree, artefacts of an institutional system set up to *create* competition and difference.

Much of what happens in the daily life of a school involves the *joint* labour of the staff and the staff's *collective* relationship to the *collective* presence of the students (their social class backgrounds, gender, ethnicity, regional culture, religion; and their current peer group life, hierarchies and exclusions, bullying, cooperation and so on). Much of the learning that school pupils do results from the shared efforts of a group of staff, from interactive learning processes among the students and, as the idea of the 'hidden curriculum' says, from the working of the institution around them.

So whether an individual teacher appears to be performing well depends a great deal on what *other* people are doing. The Standards documents, and the new generation of teacher evaluation schemes, elaborately define the 'accomplished teacher' as an individual – but say nothing about the 'accomplished department' or the 'accomplished school'. It was shown in industrial sociology, decades ago, that in the large-scale collective labour processes characteristic of the modern economy, it is impossible to measure the contribution of any *individual* worker to output. Therefore attempts to establish income differentials have become fundamentally irrational – that is, exercises in social power, not the rational determination of value. Neoliberal teacher evaluation schemes face the same paradox and cannot overcome it.

The occupation. Professionalism has been important to teachers in the past. But the idea of teaching as a profession has always been ambivalent; it enshrines dependence as much as autonomy. In neoliberal market society, professionalism is ambivalent in a new way. Definitions in the Standards documents display the complexity of teachers' work, but also enshrine the neoliberal distrust of professions. They codify teachers' work and teacher education in ways that make them auditable and allow control at a distance.

Therefore how teacher professionalism is defined, and by whom, is important. If teachers' occupational identity is defined from outside, by the power of the state or the pressure of the market, it is likely to be limited in important ways. The capacity to talk back to management, to dissent or to follow independent judgement, is not likely to bulk large in such definitions of teaching. Yet this is crucial on educational grounds, allowing teachers to pursue the interests of the pupils they actually have in front of them.

Current mainstream curriculum and assessment are largely constructed around the model of an academically engaged pupil, who will succeed on the tests. Such pupils are much more common in schools serving privileged clienteles. Teachers engaged in the education of children from other social backgrounds and with other interests need a model of professionalism that gives them room for manoeuvre, in order to teach well. We are not talking about a small group of the 'socially excluded' here, but about very large numbers of children in mainstream schools.

Good teaching is not only to a large degree collective labour, it needs also to be diverse. A well-functioning school needs a range of capabilities and performances among its teachers. Any definition of teacher quality, any system of monitoring or promotion, that tends to impose a *single* model of excellence on the teaching workforce – whatever that model may be – is likely to be damaging to the education system as a whole.

Professionalism with scope and variety needs to be supported by a lively occupational culture among teachers. Occupational culture is not a focus of current discussions of teacher quality, but it should be. It includes the shared social identity of teachers; the informal processes by which practical know-how is passed to new teachers through on-the-job learning; the occupational expertise, that is referred to in Standards statements, on which pupils rely especially when they don't come from families with advanced education; and the meta-competencies (defined below) that allow the strategic use of specific competencies.

A lively occupational culture among teachers is not a given. It needs to be fostered and it can be damaged. The market-based restructuring of technical and further education in the last generation has gone a long way to destroying the occupational culture of teaching in that sector, as the deeply depressing study by Judith Clark (2003) shows. Weber's (2007) review of international research on teachers under neoliberalism suggests widespread tension and dissatisfaction. Fostering, rather than eroding, teachers' occupational culture is likely to be important for preserving the *resilience* of teachers in the face of tough teaching situations; which as Sammons *et al.* (2007) point out in the UK, is especially important as a resource in disadvantaged schools.

An occupational culture grows out of a collective history, but it will not be a resource if it is stuck in the past. One of the significant ways in which the social situation of teachers changes is the range of situations in which they teach. This is illustrated by Ursula Hoadley's (2003) observations of two schools in post-Apartheid South Africa, one teaching in English and the other in Xhosa. With approximately double the class size and one-third of the actual instruction time for any child, the latter has to use batch methods while the former can use individual pacing. Yet it is the second school that has a stronger culture of collaboration among the teachers.

The intellectual structure of education. One of the virtues of the scholar–teacher model was its clear account of Education as a field of knowledge. The reflective-practitioner approach, though less interested in the overall organization of knowledge, has focused on how occupational knowledge can be developed in teachers' practice.

The neoliberal agenda and the competent-teacher model have abandoned these problems. The 'competencies' statements produced by the Institutes reveal no underlying idea of a field of knowledge; they are dot-point lists. The audit culture in education construes teachers as technicians, enacting pre-defined 'best practice' with a pre-defined curriculum measured against external tests. Skill, but not intelligence, is required.

I argued at the start of this chapter that teaching is a form of intellectual work. To do it well requires endless initiative and invention – the constant improvisation revealed in studies of the teaching labour process. It also requires a depth of knowledge about the culture, and a practice of critical analysis, which only an intellectually substantial program of teacher education will support.

Here we cannot afford to be nostalgic. What counts as intellectually substantial now is different from what it was in the days of Matthew Arnold or John Dewey. We now live in a world that is consciously postcolonial and post-patriarchal. The old models of knowledge on which rested both the subject curriculum in high schools and the scholar–teacher model in universities, have been subjected to compelling critiques. These include feminist analyses of patriarchal knowledge (Crowley and Himmelweit 1992) and post-modern incredulity towards the 'grand narratives' of progress and enlightenment (Lyotard 1984). As Martín Hopenhayn (2001) points out for Latin America, the rise of neoliberalism has destroyed many of the assumptions on which the social sciences previously rested. Meanwhile new frameworks of knowledge have arisen: postcolonial theory, indigenous knowledge and machine-based information systems among them. Old certainties about knowledge are gone. Educational philosophy has begun to reckon with this fundamental fact (Peters 1995); teacher education now faces the same issue.

A contemporary teacher education program has to orient itself to the world its students will actually be working in. Good teacher education is intellectually exciting. It has to be, because teachers as intellectual workers are not served by a static body of knowledge. It has been increasingly recognized that teachers in schools can and should function as their own researchers. To take just one example: in relation to ICT, both hardware and software change so fast that the training given in initial teacher education will be obsolete in just a few years. Teachers need the capacity to research emerging knowledge, techniques and machinery that we cannot possibly define in advance, and apply them to the needs of student groups that we also cannot predict.

The process of education. Education is often understood fundamentally as social reproduction – transmitting the culture to a new generation, producing the workforce, handing on the traditions or reproducing social inequalities (Bourdieu and Passeron 1977). There is some truth in these ideas; but more fundamentally still, education is a process of *forming* a culture.

Teaching is not only the training of young people in defined practices, it is about the creation of capacities for practice (Connell 1995). Education is a process that creates social reality, necessarily producing something new. Education is part of the process that steers a society through historical time; it has to do with the onto-formativity of social practice defined in the Introduction to this book. Questions about the goals of education are questions about the direction in which we want a social order to move, given that societies cannot avoid changing. This is where questions of privilege and social justice in education arise; they are fundamental to the project, not add-ons.

This reflection opens a new approach to the question of teacher competencies. Many of the problems in the 'competent teacher' model arise because of the lack of attention to the *relations between* competencies. For instance: the question of how to help teachers shift from skill set A to skill set B, when A has become obsolete; the question of the balance between technical skills in teaching an examined syllabus and the emotional labour involved in pastoral work with pupils; the failure to recognize conflicting definitions of competencies, and conflicts over who has the right to define them – managers, classroom teachers, children, parents or outside authorities.

We can say, then, that some fundamental questions about teaching concern meta-competencies, that is capacities to balance, choose among and deploy specific competencies. In the light of what we know about the teaching labour process, meta-competencies may be collective as much as they are individual.

This brings us back to the argument about why teaching matters. At the start of this chapter I quoted the OECD (2005) report on teachers. A remarkable part of the OECD's argument was the idea that teacher quality should be emphasized as a determinant of pupil outcomes because students' social background and abilities are not open to policy influence.

This is an extraordinarily blinkered perspective. Social background and student abilities *are* open to change and can be changed on a very large scale. It is a question of how a society's resources are deployed – what collective decisions are made about social steering. The global creation of mass literacy; the vast changes in girls' and women's education around the world in the last two generations; the reduction of class inequalities in access to secondary schooling – these are all examples of collective decisions about the steering of a society which profoundly changed learning outcomes.

An adequate concept of good teaching, then, includes teachers' roles in the social action required to create good learning environments for children.

We currently have good learning environments in many of the schools serving privileged classes in Australia, as in other wealthy countries. But we do not have good learning environments in most of the schools serving working-class communities and especially the most marginalized. This issue cannot be separated from teachers' responsibilities on the grounds of professional neutrality – it determines the everyday realities of teaching. Indeed, who better than teachers to know what is needed to create good learning environments for children? Teachers have a weighty responsibility here and teacher educators and education policymakers have a responsibility to support it.

6

Not the Pyramids: Intellectual Workers Today

From 1996 to 2007 Australia was governed by a right-wing coalition that made a habit of stirring up social anxiety about refugees, terrorism and Islam. On election night in October 2004 I was invited to a dinner-and-television party in an inner suburb of Sydney. Most people in the room were professionals and cultural producers of various kinds – among them an author, a musician, an academic and a human services administrator. As the voting results came in and the thumping success of that year's fear campaign became clear, the party went quiet. Eventually one of the guests remarked that she found the results surprising, because she did not know personally *anyone* who had been going to vote for the government. Others around the room nodded and said that was true for them too.

I could not say the same myself. But the conversation was striking as a measure of the distance between a regime in power and a considerable part of the intelligentsia. The hostility was reciprocated. Governments since the 1980s – not only in Australia – have set out to commercialize universities, expand corporate control of communication and culture, and discredit intellectuals who call in question the official line. In many policy fields, expert knowledge has been brushed aside as soon as it conflicted with corporate interests, the market agenda or the party line. This seems to reflect a larger cultural shift in which the uses of knowledge are at issue.

Here, for instance, are the reflections of a computer systems designer, Kieran, interviewed in the course of my research on intellectual labour:

> The twin things of globalization plus a shift to an accounting-oriented world, something that really worries me. I feel that we're losing perception of civilization.

Kieran is a technical expert in a high-technology business, who might well feel that the world is his oyster. But he also takes a broad view of culture and history. In the interview he gave examples of great engineering projects – building the Pyramids, sending a man to the moon – which had, in their time, great flow-on effects in stimulating intellectual activity. Would they be done now?

> The people who run the world now would say 'Where's the profit in that, how do we make money out of that?' And consequently it wouldn't happen. So I think we're focusing on the efficiency business, the McDonald's process, getting the process perfect. But I don't think anyone is really looking at civilization, really saying, 'What can we do that no-one's ever done before?' . . . I just feel frustrated that nobody thinks those thoughts at all.

The project in which Kieran was interviewed was part of a research agenda that asked about the character of intellectual work and the situation of intellectuals, under neoliberal globalization. In this chapter I outline some key findings.

The tale of the intellectuals

According to classic European theories, intellectuals should be ruling the world, or at least setting its agenda. The great positivist philosopher Auguste Comte, a century and a half ago, saw 'savants' as bearers of social regeneration (in alliance with women and workers). Vladimir Ilich Lenin's model of a 'vanguard' of militant intellectuals leading the working class is even more familiar. Julien Benda's (1928) *The Treason of the Intellectuals*, a best-seller in its day, argued urgently for keeping a distance from the corrupting world of political emotion. Karl Mannheim's (1929) *Ideology and Utopia*, a founding text of the sociology of knowledge, saw the independence of intellectuals as the condition not only for resolving the problem of relativism, but also for creating a scientific politics.

In the next generation these themes matured into analyses of intellectuals as a 'new class'. In critical analyses of the Soviet bloc, they were seen as the core of a new power structure (Konrád and Szelényi 1979). In the capitalist world, the growth of new technologies, large-scale corporations with their complex demands for finance and planning, nuclear weapons systems and government involvement in the economy, all seemed to give a strategic social position to the bearers of knowledge.

A very influential argument by the US sociologist Alvin Gouldner, in *The Future of Intellectuals and the Rise of the New Class* (1979), saw the growth of higher education and professional employment as producing a 'culture of critical discourse'. Intellectuals as a social force were necessarily opposed to the power of corporate capitalism. A less-known but more sophisticated analysis was produced by the Australian journal *Arena* in the 1970s and 1980s. The *Arena* group looked at the intellectually trained as a workforce and suggested that the social relations involved in intellectual work pushed this workforce towards egalitarian and socially critical views, making it a likely site of opposition under corporate capitalism (Sharp 1983). I have data to test this argument.

The idea of an oppositional new class has been adopted by many neoconservative commentators. They simply give it a different political slant, in polemics against 'political correctness' and the chardonnay-sipping 'liberal elites' who don't care for the ordinary working man.

But some sociologists have questioned the whole idea of 'the intelligentsia' as a distinctive social group, and any idea that intellectuals tend to be oppositional. Zygmunt Bauman's *Legislators and Interpreters* (1987) is sardonic about enlightenment, connecting the modern 'role' of intellectual with the rise of the modern state, rejection of popular culture, and systems of surveillance and control. Bauman suggests that with the transition to postmodernity this role is falling apart; intellectuals cannot be cultural 'legislators' any more.

There are large problems with this evolving tale, not least its Eurocentrism. Yet similar questions about the role of intellectuals in social change have been raised outside the global metropole. Ali Shariati (1986) in Iran proposed a sociology of intellectuals that gave a key role to *rushanfekr*, thinkers with a close connection to the people, but without a claim to power, who were able to offer interpretations of their time and their society. More recently there have been vehement debates about the role of indigenous knowledge, and Northern-trained intellectuals, in postcolonial Africa (Mkandawire 2005).

What is an intellectual?

In this chapter I draw on the findings of two research projects in Australia. One was a close-focus study in which 58 people from four fields of intellectual labour were interviewed about their lives and careers, during 1997–8. The second was a cross-sectional telephone survey of 500 intellectual workers, drawn from forty occupational categories and all states, conducted in April–June 2000.

In the life-history study we interviewed research scientists, applied scientists, policymakers, journalists, management consultants, software designers, authors, philosophers and clergy, among others. Very few were comfortable with the term 'intellectual'. When we explained the nature of our study, the commonest response was, 'why me?' 'Intellectual' is not a popular identity to claim.

But all of these people were doing intellectual work and for most of them, cultural production or the gathering and application of knowledge was the main part of their business. I think the *Arena* group had it right: it is intellectual *work* that is the core of the matter. To be an intellectual – at least at this stage of history – is to be one of a group performing a particular kind of labour and requiring certain kinds of resources.

Our image of the intellectual tends to focus on great minds and great breakthroughs – Einstein, Darwin, Ibsen. Some of the people in our life-history study did tell about great moments in their own lives, when a new research field opened up, a deep shift in ideas occurred or a book-writing task began to 'flow'. Nevertheless, most intellectual work is routine, whether assembling information or interpreting it, generating cultural materials, performing or disseminating them. One of our respondents, looking back at her experience in a university research laboratory, remarked bitterly:

> Look, a well-trained monkey can do this work.

That was a biochemist with a PhD. In our cross-sectional survey, respondents were asked which of these statements best characterized their work:

> *My work mainly involves solving problems by applying existing ideas, knowledge or methods.*

> *My work mainly involves trying to produce new ideas, knowledge or methods.*

Across the whole sample, 54 per cent said the former, 43 per cent the latter. Of course this varies from field to field, with the former response more common in obviously 'applied' fields.

We need to think of what intellectuals do as a *labour process*; and consider, as we would for any other group of workers, the conditions of this labour and the organization of the workforce.

Intellectual labour

Details of the work obviously vary, but there are common elements. For instance, among those whose work involves knowledge about social relations, there seem to be two basic intellectual processes in their daily routines. The first might be called 'making a warranted statement'. This is essentially the process identified in Latour and Woolgar's (1979) famous ethnography _Laboratory Life_ in their analysis of peptide chemistry. The second might be called 'making a warranted decision'. Here for instance is Patrick, a psychiatrist, describing how he makes a patient assessment:

> Well, first is to find out what problems need to be dealt with and essentially you ask them, or somebody tells you that they need to be assessed because of particular behaviour. First of all, as in any psychiatric admission unit, your history-taking is based around the presenting behaviour and related material. Then, having dealt with that, it gives you further clues as to what other areas that you need to delve into – background, family relationships, family history, past psychiatric history, all of that. Having got those related areas, then you sort of fill out the picture, getting social information, early development history, that sort of thing. Then you make your diagnosis and then you make your management plan.

Patrick assembles specific information about the case, gathers new information that he judges to be required, and then follows the professionally defined decision-making procedure. At all stages he is applying his technical knowledge, for instance his background knowledge of what constitute 'clues' and what information is needed in a case history.

These processes are, of course, subject to historical change. And a strong sense of change came through in both the life-history study and the survey. In response to the statement _In my field of work, knowledge and methods are changing rapidly_, no less than 83 per cent of survey respondents agreed and only 15 per cent disagreed.

The most striking recent change is the advent of computer technology. Though there were many individual differences, our respondents were collectively heavy users of information and communication technology (ICT). In the cross-sectional survey, 94 per cent described themselves as 'regularly' using a personal computer,

89 per cent as 'regularly' using email, 73 per cent as 'regularly' using the Internet. These were impressive levels of penetration, ten years ago, and they were spread fairly evenly across fields and sectors. Some respondents, extremely sophisticated users of ICT, gave us detailed narratives of the transformation of specific fields of knowledge work by new technologies.

Does computer technology change the nature of intellectual work? No computer is yet able to do what Patrick does, and there are other intellectual processes that are little affected. But in some forms of intellectual work there seems to be a basic change.

The capacities of databases and retrieval systems are changing the nature of expertise. In an earlier generation, being a scholar meant having read (and being able to remember and sort) an immense amount of detail about one's subject. That is exactly the job computers do best. Ideally, then, every scholar's intellectual power would now be amplified, the time spent on simple reading and retrieving would be reduced, while leisure and reflection would rise.

But that is not happening. For one thing, time isn't saved. Hours of work continue to be long. Respondents in the cross-sectional survey reported an average working week of about fifty hours. There is more sense of growing pressure than of intellectual spaciousness.

For instance Elaine, a senior academic in the humanities, feels acutely the loss of the leisure required for reading. She struggles to keep up with the journals in her field, loses ground, and so from time to time sends her research assistant to conduct electronic 'raids' on the literature. Elaine considers that the change has penetrated the core process of producing knowledge in her field, the writing of technical papers:

> It's got less and less to do with communication and more and more to do with establishing credentials . . . That's the big change that I've seen. It's not about communication. Once it used to be – the business of writing . . . reading one another's draft and then reading the journal. It's part of a different exercise. We're producing parcels of information, that I don't think a lot of us are reading.

Here, Elaine appeals to an older intellectual technology – the world of seminars, face-to-face discussions and cycles of debate and reflection. Some of our respondents recalled with great affection their days of excited discussion in smoke-filled pubs or cutting-edge laboratories where the latest theories and techniques were hotly debated. But they located these experiences well in the past and often on the other side of the world.

ICT has also penetrated these processes of peer exchange and communities of knowledge. Email communication is now so much a part of standard practice that it is hardly noticed how much it is used. In the business world, labour processes involving knowledge are now extensively integrated with computer systems. Rachel, a senior manager at a financial services firm, starts the day early:

> I'm linked every which way you possibly can: fax, Internet, email, so I'll do a lot at home . . . Technology plays a very big part of my job . . . I'm an absolute news hound and I love getting up, I mean I get up at 5 o'clock every day, because I'm an early morning person and I hit the Internet and I read the *Financial Times* and the *Sydney Morning Herald* and CNN and get the World News, I love it, it's at my fingertips.

Contemporary market research and management consultancy practice would be inconceivable without computer technology.

Across a range of fields, ICT has made possible a new level of collectivization in the intellectual labour process. To understand contemporary intellectual life, then, we must look carefully at its institutional setting.

Workplace and sector

Though there is still a significant number who work independently – some 19 per cent of the respondents in our survey were in a personal practice or a small partnership – the great majority of contemporary intellectual workers are employees in organizations.

These include universities, government agencies, corporations, large partnerships and voluntary sector organizations.

The *Arena* thesis suggests we might find in this organizational life some structural bases for a democratic outlook. At first sight, our data seem to refute this. Asked if there is a specific person who supervises their work, 61 per cent of respondents in the survey say there is. Asked if they supervise other employees, 78 per cent say that they do. A majority, then, appear to be in a hierarchical workplace, much like other workers.

However our respondents do not have a strong perception of being in a hierarchical setting. On the contrary, when asked to respond to the statement *Most people in my workplace treat each other as equals*, some 81 per cent agreed and only 14 per cent disagreed. Here the *Arena* thesis seems better supported. There is a sense of equality within the intellectual workplace and there is a good deal of networking in it and beyond it. The high usage of email is relevant here, as this is a technology well adapted for peer-group communication. Our life histories have many examples of intellectual peer groups and 'invisible colleges'.

However this does not readily turn into an oppositional consciousness. There is, for instance, only a modest rate of unionization. Among respondents to our survey, just 28 per cent are members of a union – compared with 64 per cent who are members of a professional association. The stronger tendency among our respondents seems to be a sense of individual empowerment, of personal autonomy. To the statement *I have a high level of autonomy or independence in the work that I do*, no less than 95 per cent agreed – 49 per cent 'strongly'.

Though an emphasis on the personal autonomy of intellectual workers is the dominant note, the institutional setting does matter. Indeed, institutional setting is clearly associated with this sense of autonomy itself. We developed a seven-item scale to measure the 'autonomy' factor, and institutional sector was clearly associated with this variable. Workers in the university and government sectors had the *lowest* 'autonomy' scores. (Evidently, whatever we have left of academic freedom does not produce unusual independence for university workers.) When we looked at opinions on issues of cultural politics, including support for the neoliberal market agenda itself, sector of employment and level of unionization were important predictors of attitudes.

In a number of ways, our data show the importance of organizational context in the lives of intellectual workers. This has two theoretical implications. On the one hand, it argues against the thesis, common in postmodernist texts, that culture has somehow become autonomous, floating free of material determinations. On the other hand, it argues against the 'convergence' thesis, that corporate and academic cultures have merged. They *may* be converging, but they are far from identical at this point.

Quasi-globalization

A main problem about the older tale of the intellectuals is its geopolitical naivety. Intelligentsias are not simply local. Our respondents in both studies have impressive levels of international connection. For a considerable number, the crucial event in their careers was travel to another country and study or work outside Australia. For a good many, a continuing connection with colleagues in other countries is crucial to the work they do.

There are of course differences in the level of international involvement. We were able to construct quantitative scales to measure this and an important and unexpected result emerged. Contrary to the widespread idea that we are being globalized under the impact of market forces, it is not corporate sector intellectual workers who show the highest levels of international engagement. It is university workers.

But the connections are not fully global. Consider this discussion of inter-departmental contacts by Terry, a professor in chemistry. In his field, he says,

> Well, there's quite a close knit – there's no formal structure, but quite a close knit association between, particularly [departments] in the UK and United States and Canada and New Zealand for that matter. But

also to a lesser extent but still nevertheless quite useful, with quite a few of the European countries like France and Germany in particular and Holland. There's a like a network, exchange of information about all aspects of [field] education. And of course a lot of these people linked each others' international conferences, which is clearly an important part of it.

The countries Terry mentions are the rich countries of the First World, principally North America and western Europe. That is absolutely typical. Most of our respondents hardly register this stark cultural and economic bias. 'International science' or 'international connections' generally mean connections with the global metropole, not with global society generally. When developing countries figure at all in Australian intellectual workers' stories, it is likely to be as recipients of aid or targets of intervention – not as sources of knowledge, wisdom or innovation.

We are, then, not so much globalized as quasi-globalized. Many of the strategic issues in Australian intellectual workers' careers concern participation from, not in, the periphery. One still gets kudos in Australian intellectual life mainly by getting recognized in the metropole. And one cannot normally get this by email. The basic moves are still the old techniques of personal contact – travel to the centre, doing higher degrees at Oxbridge or the Ivy League, doing a training course in the parent company, doing a tour of duty in head office and making a splash there, giving papers at international conferences, visiting laboratories in Germany. Electronic peer contacts build on those personal links, they do not yet substitute for them.

So globalization, as experienced by Australian intellectual workers, is not an opening-up of the world to a boundary-free cross-fertilization of cultures and knowledges. It is still a process dominated by the institutions and knowledge systems of the global metropole. Though there are individual exceptions, collectively the Australian intelligentsia participates in the world through its relationship with metropolitan culture. This is specifically relevant to Australian views of Islam. In the course of our life-history interviewing, across a range of fields and institutions, we met no one

who had done any of their training in a Muslim majority country
or for whom Islam was a significant cultural force.

Conclusion: intellectual workers' place in the world

Among our respondents who work for corporations, no tension
between the power of knowledge and the power of command
is visible. The capacity to deploy intellectual techniques is itself
a major resource in managerial careers, in Australia and doubtless
elsewhere. In such careers an intellectual identity is difficult to
sustain. Some respondents locate their intellectual excitement at
an earlier stage of their career, some shift their intellectual interests
into private life (describing, for instance, a pile of books by the
bedside).

The nearest thing to a managerial/intellectual identity is the
'strategic advisor' role, played by two people we interviewed,
both women. Both were outside the line-management hierarchy
and both have an unusually broad, reflective view of the world of
corporations and state power. But not a critical view.

In the academic world, a critical view is more easily taken and
neoliberal attitudes are less common. In our cross-sectional survey,
on a measure of market ideology, university-based respondents
were the most oppositional of all sectors, corporate employees the
most market-oriented. That is a robust statistical finding. But it
did not mean that academics boasted a confident intellectual identity. On a measure of cultural optimism (vs cultural pessimism),
university-based respondents scored relatively low and corporate
respondents relatively high.

Some reasons for cultural pessimism emerge in the life-history
interviews. As one respondent – a part-time lecturer, part-time
journalist – remarks, 'there's no secure place. Universities are
not secure, newspapers certainly aren't secure.' Bertrand, a
full-time academic, focuses on the changes inside universities
that have accompanied commercialization and corporate-style
management:

My sense as a lecturer back in the 'seventies and 'eighties was that we *were* the university. When you thought of it, it was this big body of people and then a group of others who were supportive, like Vice-Chancellors and so on . . . Whereas my sense now is that that has all changed, turned around. And you are very conscious of someone else running the university and they don't appear particularly friendly. Although they readily say things that are intended to keep people feeling possibly relaxed and comfortable, but have anything but that effect.

Among some respondents – though certainly not all – there is a sense of full-blown cultural crisis around the role of an academic; a sense that a valuable way of life has been destroyed and nothing very admirable has taken its place.

Kieran, whom I quoted at the start of this paper, isn't quite right that 'nobody thinks those thoughts at all'. There are still many who do think large thoughts about civilization and the long-term future. But the circumstances of the thinking have certainly changed. There is a widespread sense among our respondents, in both studies, that the ground has shifted, that older modes of intellectual work are passing or have already passed. Among some respondents there is marked insecurity. Among many there is a sense of being under pressure, which often takes the form of a shortage of time, to do all that they should be doing.

The pressure for change does not, on the face of it, come from globalization. Indeed, the pattern of international connection I have called 'quasi-globalization' – dependence on the metropole – seems one of the more stable features of Australian intellectual life. It would be good to have more *global* globalization! But globalization has also become one of the code-words for market dominance and that certainly is a pressure producing change.

Australian intellectual workers, examined empirically, do not look very much like the 'new class' of either progressive theory or new-right journalism. But neither do they look like the bearers of free-floating postmodern culture. They are mostly working in organizations and performing an increasingly collectivized form of labour. They remain a group in which oppositional ideas exist, but they are institutionally divided, unlikely to act as a coherent cultural force.

Are there alternatives? We were able to identify statistically a group who are relatively marginalized from the organizational mainstream and who show high levels of autonomy in their work. We might speculate that the organizational strategy of casualizing the intellectual workforce will produce alienation and opposition in the future. But most intellectual workers are still in the organizational world.

Here a key issue is the growing tension between market-oriented managerialism and the culturally embedded concerns of intellectual workers for the quality of their own work, for collegiality in the workplace, and for the right to pursue truth wherever the search leads. I doubt those will ever be the banners of a revolution, but they are 'values' that will increasingly matter to other social groups as well. Intellectual workers might then become, not a 'vanguard' in the old sense, but pioneers for moves beyond neoliberalism.

Those are long-term possibilities. For the moment, intellectual workers in Australia are not a powerful force for change. Those who are closest to the levers of power are those who are least likely to dissent from the reigning ethos of neoliberalism and its emphasis on short-term advantage. For the time being, Kieran is mostly right about the pyramids.

7

Sociology has a World History

All societies have ways of identifying social groups and describing social relations. There is some archaeological evidence that social symbolism emerged around forty thousand years ago. It appeared in cave paintings and carvings about the time anatomically modern humans (*homo sapiens sapiens*) spread around the world. This was, according to Jane Balme and Sandra Bowdler (2006), part of the process of creating the divisions of labour, such as gender, and the sustained forms of social cooperation, such as food sharing, that underpin the societies we know in history.

In more recent history, as Vere Gordon Childe (1960) famously argued, a growing division of labour allowed specialized artisans and then, in urban societies, intellectuals and writing. It became possible to formalize a language for talking about social order and to speculate about the shape social relations should take. The social philosophy of Kong Fuzi's *Analects*, the political analysis of Ibn Khaldun's *Muqaddimah*, the gender critique of Christine de Pizan's *City of Women*, became possible.

About a hundred and twenty years ago, in Europe and eastern North America, something new happened that produced 'sociology' as an organized cultural practice – a 'science', as its advocates named it. What had happened? In the story told by most introductory-sociology textbooks, what happened was European and North American modernity: the industrial revolution, democracy, bureaucracy and secularization. A small group of brilliant intellectuals, especially Marx, Durkheim and Weber, interpreted this change and thus became the Founding Fathers of sociology and the authors of Classical Theory.

We might say that the discipline has an *internalist* account of its own origin. Some years ago I wrote a long essay, 'Why is classical theory classical?' (Connell 1997), that raised severe doubts about this story.

First, the making of sociology was a collective enterprise, as writers of textbooks at the end of the nineteenth century emphasized, not the invention of three or even six founding fathers. The collective work required means of coordination, including the textbooks themselves. Newly founded periodicals, conferences and associations were involved. The language of 'social science', devised by the philosopher Auguste Comte in the first half of the century, was taken up soon after his death in the 1850s by a broad spectrum of reformers. A generation later, more specialized or academic bodies such as the *Institut International de Sociologie* and the American Sociological Society were created.

Second, claiming the title of 'science' implied, to Victorian minds, speculative generalizations supported by a large body of information. Therefore the recording and classification of social knowledge became a major part of the enterprise. Works such as Herbert Spencer's immensely influential *Principles of Sociology*, published in the 1870s, took the form of huge accumulations of little descriptions of social institutions, customs and events. Investigations of social conditions in the metropole certainly went into this brew. But the gaze of Spencer, Ward, Engels, Letourneau, Tönnies, Durkheim, Sumner, Giddings, Hobhouse and their colleagues ranged far beyond the metropole. They gathered and incorporated vast amounts of data from the colonized world.

Third, the conceptual framework of sociology was based on the contrast between metropole and colony. The distinction of 'primitive' from 'advanced' social forms underpinned the concept of social progress that governed the new science for its first two generations. The doctrine of progress gave the liberal intellectuals who created sociology a solution to the cultural dilemma they faced, as beneficiaries of imperialism. In the Comtean universe, sociology was the universal 'mother science' (Anderson 1912), of which specific sciences such as economics were the children. Assembling data from all societies allowed the claim to rigorous scientificity. By the 1890s, it was these data and this claim that marked 'sociology' off from the vague moral discourse of social improvement so widespread in the generation before. In substance and in framing, I argued, sociology was global from the start.

This argument was not received with universal joy. Indeed, the *American Journal of Sociology*, which kindly published my essay, took the unusual step of publishing an attack on it, called 'A sociological guilt trip', in the same issue (Collins 1997). Other scholars have offered more sober defences of the 'classical theory' story (Baehr 2002). More detailed research on intellectual history has certainly shown that my account was too schematic. The timing of events among French-speaking sociologists, for instance, is different from that among the English-speaking (Steinmetz 2011).

But the fundamental point, I think, has been strongly established. Sociology as a science is not a product of an internal evolution within 'modern' Europe and North America. As a collective practice, sociology emerged in a context of global imperialism, it embedded intellectual responses to empire, and its history has to be understood in a world context.

Making professional sociology: the changing metropole/periphery relationship

To acknowledge that sociology was always global does not imply that its global-ness was static. Since the structures of world society have been in upheaval in the last hundred years, there is every reason to expect that the metropole/periphery relationship within sociology would also change. I see this relationship developing through three phases.

Sociology came into existence at the high tide of European imperialism and offered a synthesis of the liberal bourgeoisie's consciousness of worldwide empire. The relationship was very much that defined in Hountondji's (1995) observations on the global structure of scientific knowledge. Metropole and colony had distinct functions. Theory-making was located in the metropole. Data-gathering, and some applications of science at the end of the process, occurred in the colonized world. Data from the frontier of conquest, exploration and trade were collected by travellers, missionaries, military officers and colonial administrators and savants. The footnotes and bibliographies of sociology texts, from the 1870s to the Great War, overflow with references to their reports.

In time, data collection in the periphery became professionalized. Ethnography, as a fieldwork and writing genre, was born, installing in the human sciences the natural-science model of full-time remote data-collector. Social-scientific data archives were created – private, official and academic. (Herbert Spencer compiled one of the first.) The colonial state, in the nineteenth-century regularization of colonial rule, had a growing appetite for intelligence about its subject populations. Census-taking became more systematic, and the alliance between colonial administration and anthropology was born, though its full flowering came a little later (Asad 1973).

The theory of progress, and the science called sociology that embodied it, could be exported from the metropole to the periphery. Spencer's sociology was read, and by some enthusiastically adopted, in Meiji Japan and colonized Bengal. Comte's positivism was taken up, notably, in Brazil, where Comtean temples of humanity were built and where a Comtean sociological slogan – ORDEN Y PROGRESO – is still emblazoned on the Republic's national flag. It was possible for intellectuals in the colonies, before or after independence, to share in the writing of sociology, by participating in the metropolitan attempt to characterize progress.

Early in the new century the European cultural crisis that was undermining the rationale of empire spread to sociology. By the 1920s Comtean sociology was in full retreat and by the end of that decade it was gone. I think we can speak, in Althusser's terminology, of an epistemological break occurring in metropolitan social science. It is not an accident that this happened at the time of the political crisis of North Atlantic/ European imperialism. With war in the metropole, the collapse of three empires, and social revolution, the concept of progress lost its power to frame the thought of the metropolitan intelligentsia.

In the debris of Comtean sociology, a magma of possible successors bubbled. Among them were the sociology of knowledge, various syntheses of Freud with Marx, cultural-relativist speculations and a social theory of gender. One of the most dramatic eruptions in this magma was the 'system of sociology' published by the Bolshevik theorist Nikolai Bukharin (1925). Bukharin adopted a practically Comtean definition of sociology, but gave it a revolutionary-socialist content. Among his themes was equilibrium and disequilibrium between society and nature, giving some of his writing a strikingly contemporary ring.

But Bukharin went the way of most of Stalin's opponents – he was shot in 1938. Many of his contemporaries, including Mannheim and Vaerting, lost their jobs or their homes under the dictatorships. By 1940 the main institutional base left for sociology was the US university system, though the emerging welfare states of Britain and Scandinavia also offered possibilities (Wisselgren 2000). In the United States, sociology found an identity, no longer as the 'mother science', but as one sibling among others. It survived in an academic division of labour alongside departments of political science, economics, history and anthropology.

Conflict and differentiation *within the society of the metropole* now became the main themes of sociology. A connection, both institutional and intellectual, developed with the welfare state and its compromise with corporate capital. Karl Mannheim's writing after his exile from Germany is a major example. It ranged from the urgent exploration of crisis, irrationality and dictatorship in *Mensch und Gesellschaft im Zeitalter des Umbaus* (1935 – somewhat palely translated as 'Man and Society in an Age of Reconstruction') to the Keynesian sociology of *Freedom, Power and Democratic Planning* (1951).

Empirical sociology too looked for solutions to social tensions, funded by corporations, corporate foundations and the state. This was a highly creative moment for sociology, purely in terms of method: rapid development occurred in urban ethnography, life-history method, social analysis of census data, sample surveys and attitude scaling, and mathematical analysis of census data. These developments crystallized what Burawoy (2005) has recently defined as 'professional' and 'policy' sociology, with figures like William Ogburn and Paul Lazarsfeld as leaders.

Almost all these methods were focused inwards on the society of the metropole. A methodological tendency to define the society of the metropole as a world unto itself was reinforced by a shift in theory towards the idea of a 'social system'. By the 1950s Talcott Parsons' systems theory formed the major paradigm in metro-politan sociology. Now the boundedness of a social order was a taken-for-granted assumption. Through the first half of the twentieth century, then, sociology in the metropole, especially the USA and Britain, turned decisively away from the periphery.

Yet metropolitan sociology continued to be haunted by the periphery. French sociologists maintained more of the earlier interest and a full-scale sociology of colonies was written by René Maunier (1932), attempting to theorize a fundamentally divided society. In the Nazi time, as George Steinmetz (2011) shows, those sociologists who stayed in Germany were recruited to work on colonial policy. After the war in the USA, systems theory laid some foundations for what was to become modernization theory. Even Parsons, at the end of his career, re-discovered social evolution.

During the cold war, the US state and corporate leadership tried to implant 'western' social science in developing countries. Students were brought to US universities, departments were funded and research grants provided in their home countries. For a time, the Ford Foundation became the largest financial supporter of social science research in Latin America and the Rockefeller Foundation was also involved in setting up social science in sub-Saharan Africa (Berman 1983).

This contact created some interest in decolonization, in US sociology, but had little impact on sociological method or theory. In the late twentieth century, research methods went through an unprecedented technologization. This included automated factor analysis, computer-assisted telephone interviewing, survey data banks, qualitative analysis programs and Web-based research. Sociological research therefore increasingly depended on institutional wealth. A new practice of standardized multi-country studies developed, almost always funded and managed from the metropole.

Sociological theorists in the metropole, meanwhile, continued to generate universalized frameworks for understanding social action, social structure or social system. In this respect Bourdieu, Luhmann, Coleman and Giddens carried forward the generalizing enterprise of Parsons' heyday. When metropolitan theory did locate its claims in time – for instance in theories of post-industrialism, risk society, reflexive modernity, panopticism and postmodernity – this was usually presented as a sequence of development within the society of the metropole, without any reference to the historical experience of the colonized.

When sociology of this kind was implanted in the periphery, the result was an apparatus of knowledge with inbuilt tensions. Sociologists in the periphery were tied to the metropole as the source of their main methods and concepts and often by their personal careers. Yet their data were local, their students were local, their policy and public audiences were local, and in the richer parts of the periphery, such as Australia, most of their funding was local.

The hegemony of the metropole's sociology thus produced a bifurcated sociology in the periphery. This might mean no more than an exaggerated separation of method and theory from data and application. But I think the effects are more profound. They include a kind of epistemological drift where the society of the periphery comes to be understood as an imperfect extension of metropolitan modernity. That is, precisely, how most sociological theories of globalization work.

There is, therefore, a profound difficulty in connecting disciplinary sociology with the distinctive social experiences of the colonized and postcolonial world. But sociology has multiple forms. For the most creative social analyses of the periphery, we must look beyond professional sociology.

Theorizing global domination: the public sociology of the periphery

As empires expanded, an upsurge of social analysis followed. Wherever it was possible, colonized people themselves began to generate analyses of the invasion and its consequences. As I tried to show in *Southern Theory* (Connell 2007), the intellectuals of post-colonial or neocolonial societies have continued the discussion, and their work is now a tremendous resource for social thought.

To follow this discussion we need to expand the definition of what counts as sociology. Margaret Jolly (2008) has called attention to genealogy, visual art, textiles and other local genres in articulating indigenous social experience in the Pacific islands. There are powerful reasons why the intellectual production of the periphery would take distinctive forms. The intellectual structure of sociology in the metropole was one, especially its defining colonized people as primitive and its almost total indifference to the intellectuals of the periphery.

Conditions within the colonized world also shaped the forms of knowledge. A colonized society, as Georges Balandier (1955) points out, is a society in crisis. Among the desperate situations familiar across the colonized world are genocidal violence, epidemic disease, the destruction of institutions, the seizure of land, the destruction of habitats and food supplies, enslavement, the forced movement of populations, the re-structuring of gender relations and sexuality, the disruption of education, and powerful attacks on local religion.

A social catastrophe of that order is not likely to lead to a contemplative social science among indigenous people. Nor did colonies of settlement produce a settled intellectual life for the first century or two. Indeed some, including Australia, became famously anti-intellectual.

Yet many intellectuals of the colonized world were dealing with the issues that sociologists addressed. A notable example is Sun Yat-sen's *Three Principles of the People (San Min Chu I)* (1927), a set of lectures that are, in a sense, Sun's final message to the Chinese people. They offer a brilliant overview of the world of imperialism – population movements, interventionist states, economic domination, imperial rivalry and war. They trace the disintegrating effects of these forces on culture and politics in China.

In developing his analysis and his proposals for the future, Sun deals with such sociological themes as social hierarchy, bureaucracy, cultural change, education, industrial organization, embodiment and relations between society and the natural environment. On some issues, Sun seems ahead of sociological thought in the metropole in the 1920s. The genre in which he is writing, however, is not a sociological treatise, but an urgent argument about the direction for Chinese nationalist politics.

Or consider the analysis of gender relations offered by Kartini in Java in 1899–1903, under Dutch colonial rule (Kartini 2005). Kartini also reflected on the relation between European and local culture, criticized the racism of the colonizers and sought local reform and modernization. Unlike Sun's, her argument focused on the position of women. She developed a critique of the situation of women in Javanese Muslim society and proposed an agenda of change, centring on new educational institutions. The main genre of Kartini's writing was correspondence. Her letters were collected and published and became famous, after her premature death.

As these two examples suggest, many intellectuals of the colonized world were actively engaged with the culture of the colonizers. Sun, for one, read metropolitan Marxist literature and offered an interesting critique of it. Kartini's correspondence (at least the published part of it) was exchanged with progressive intellectuals in the Netherlands.

Others, however, were not, and tension developed around this. In the 1880s Sayyid Jamal ad-Din al-Afghani, one of the most influential of modern Islamic thinkers, was sharply critical of the *ulama*, the traditional Muslim intelligentsia, for remaining stuck in traditional pedagogy and failing to adopt the colonizers' knowledge (al-Afghani 1968). That particular debate has continued for the next hundred and thirty years.

One of the main tasks undertaken by intellectuals of the colonized world was to study why their societies had succumbed to invasion or economic domination. This was not an easy thing to do, unless one adopted the colonizer's point of view. The colonizers offered all too many explanations, from moral weakness to institutional primitivism. Al-Afghani understood religious culture as the key battlefield. The colonizers were bent on undermining Islam, and Islam was the necessary basis of resistance, yet religion had decayed. Al-Afghani saw the path to revival in recovering the rationalist and scientific tradition within Islam, and this too has proved an influential move.

In other parts of the world, the analysis took a different shape. In colonies of settlement, the land was strategic. Accordingly, land rights for indigenous people have become a political focus, and the struggle for land has long been an intellectual focus. It was, for instance, the centre of Solomon Plaatje's great work *Native Life in South Africa* (1916), in which religion hardly figured except as a subject for irony about the faith of the colonizers. This was a mixed-genre book that included the results of embattled fieldwork with displaced families.

Though the focus of analysis differed from one part of the world to another, everywhere intellectuals had the task of contesting the abuse of colonized peoples. It is hard for people in the metropole to appreciate the ferocious and sustained condemnation of colonized peoples under imperialism, though this has been well documented by historians (Kiernan 1969; Anderson 2007). The contemporary racial hierarchies in Latin America (Nascimento 2007) indicate how deeply entrenched such patterns became.

Cultural movements such as *négritude* in literature and 'African philosophy' have developed in response. Mahatma Gandhi's strategy of resistance to the British Empire in India re-validated Indian popular culture, especially popular religion, as no previous nationalism had managed to do (Nandy 1983). Jomo Kenyatta, astonishingly, contested British disdain by adopting the strict method of ethnography: writing a book, *Facing Mount Kenya* (1938), that was both a fine anthropological monograph and a nationalist tract.

After decolonization, or in countries which had not been formally colonized, imperial rule was not at issue but cultural domination was. In Al-e Ahmad's (1962) witty and scathing account of 'westoxication' in Iran, there was no formal sociology. But there was a great deal of acute social observation, some of it based on fieldwork in the countryside. Al-e Ahmad worked his observations up into a subtle social psychology of individual alienation and collective malaise.

Though the religious context is very different, this had many resonances with Octavio Paz's *Labyrinth of Solitude* (1st edn 1950; for discussion see Kozlarek 2009). In this famous text Paz meditated on the limits of the Mexican revolution, the imperfect incorporation of indigenous peasantry into the national culture, the difference from European and US culture and, again, alienation in personal life. In Paz's later essay 'The Other Mexico', written after the 1968 Tlatelolco massacre, there is an angry critique of the ruling party, of development ideology and of the corruption of language in the interest of the dominant class.

Paz's writing presupposed the situation of economic dependence which became the subject of Latin America's most celebrated contribution to social science. Prebisch's analysis of capitalism in the periphery, Cardoso and Faletto's *Dependency and Development in Latin America*, and the Marxist theorists of underdevelopment, are perhaps so well known that they do not need description here. (For a lucid English-language review see Kay 1989.) Everything we could wish for in public sociology was here: debates carried out in a blaze of publicity, intellectuals interacting with social movements and political forces, and the highest possible stakes in the world of practice.

Looking back on this era, Manuel Garretón (2000) observes that sociology had the highest hopes, thinking it had found a unification of knowledge and the practice of social change. But this did not last. The unification was destroyed by the dictatorships and by the triumph of neoliberalism. By the 1990s there was great difficulty in re-establishing a Latin American critical discourse about society.

Garretón's argument shows – as Cardoso and Faletto had done in different terms thirty years before – that there is no fixed status of postcolonial, dependent or peripheral society. Rather there is a complex and evolving social history. The changes set up by colonization do not stop with independence.

This has recently been confirmed in the Pacific. Epeli Hau'ofa's *We Are the Ocean* (2008) is another demonstration of the way public sociology in the periphery crosses genres. In his work, social analysis is mixed not only with literature but also with visual art. In his essay 'The New South Pacific Society' Hau'ofa traces the gradual formation, across the inter-island distances, of a unified regional society. In this formation, the privileged groups of the different island countries, clustered around the postcolonial state, corporate businesses and aid agencies, are coming together as a regional ruling class sharing a modernized international culture. Meanwhile indigenous culture is increasingly the preserve of the poor and powerless.

How to respond to these transformations is the issue everywhere. There is no more agreement now than there was in al-Afghani's day. Broadly, the more optimistic are those who see the postcolonial subordination of the periphery in cultural or social-psychological terms. Al-e Ahmad sought an alliance of secular and religious oppositions; Hau'ofa responded by setting up an arts centre; Freire responded with an educational programme.

Those who have focused on the material exploitation or backwardness of the periphery have had a harder time, since the CEPAL strategy of import–replacement industrialization came to grief in the 1970s. Perhaps this debate too is opening again, around the industrial development of China and India. So far it is economists rather than sociologists who have made the running (Sen 1999).

Towards a multi-coloured sociology

The most obvious way to contest the dominance of Northern sociology is to assert local alternatives, as autonomous forms of knowledge. This yields what I would call a mosaic epistemology. With a mosaic epistemology, sociological knowledge consists of an array of distinct systems of concepts and data, grounded in local cultural traditions and local experience. In the best case, these systems are able to speak to each other through translations and epitomes.

This is, more or less, the epistemology implied in the discussion about 'indigenous sociology' launched by the International Sociological Association in the 1980s. Akinsola Akiwowo's (1980, 1986) argument for African perspectives in sociology, and his attempt to provide social theory generated from Yoruba oral poetry, is a notable example. It is one of the few attempts to show how indigenous sociology might work at the level of theory. This has continued to interest African sociologists as a model for the future (Adesina 2002).

However, few of the people who developed a public sociology around resistance to colonialism or postcolonial domination have adopted a mosaic epistemology. Intellectuals as prominent as al-Afghani, Sun, Fanon, Shariati and Prebisch all argued for appropriating and modifying the knowledge of the metropole, not for moving completely outside it.

Why a mosaic epistemology cannot work is shown particularly clearly in the African debates around indigenous philosophy. Without going into the detail of a complex conflict, I am persuaded by Paulin Hountondji's (1983) argument that the supposed autochthonous 'African philosophy', retrieved from folk wisdom, is neither fully autochthonous nor good philosophy. It is a representation by intellectuals that actually reproduces the colonizers' gaze on indigenous culture. It functions in the postcolonial world as ideology, often justifying the dominance of local elites and offering a 'philosophy in the third person' rather than accepting direct intellectual responsibility (Hountondji 1983; see chapter 8 below).

Bibi Bakare-Yusuf (2003) makes a powerful supporting argument, in a debate about the same problem in gender theory. A mosaic epistemology assumes that indigenous African cultures are silos – closed systems with a separate logic. That is, of course, the traditional view in Western anthropology, the basis of old-style ethnography. But it is simply not true of pre-colonial West African societies, which were dynamic social orders, open to change, constantly interacting with each other and with influences from other world regions.

It seems to me, in the light of these debates, that the future for world social science does not lie with a mosaic model. But we cannot fall back on the default option of an endless extension of metropolitan hegemony in the name of universal science. Many of those who have pondered the shape of world sociology seem to have arrived at the same opinion (e.g. Martin and Beittel 1998; Alatas 2006). It is the common ground of two international collections published in 2010, Sujata Patel's *ISA Handbook of Diverse Sociological Traditions* and *Facing an Unequal World: Challenges for a Global Sociology*, edited by Michael Burawoy, Mau-kuei Chang and Michelle Fei-yu Hsieh. Where do we go from here?

Central to the work of all of the intellectuals discussed in the previous section was something that has remained marginal in metropolitan sociology. That is the colonial conquest itself, and the cultural and intellectual encounters it has created. The responsibility accepted by those intellectuals was to make, out of these encounters, a response to colonialism and postcolonial domination.

In the history of these responses, I believe, we will find the key resources for a multi-centred world sociology. Not only will this be culturally richer than metropolitan sociology – hence I call it 'multi-coloured'. Social science of this kind can play a unique democratic role in a neoliberal world.

The field of social science where this process has gone furthest, as far as I know, is gender research. Many people think this is a new theme in social science, but it is not. Gender was an important theme in Comtean sociology, more than a hundred years ago. Some first-wave feminists were social scientists; the feminist educator Mathilde Vaerting published the first fully developed social theory of gender in 1921. Gender remained an issue in internalist sociology in the metropole, even for men; no less a figure than Talcott Parsons published papers on the subject in the 1940s and a book in 1956. Gender as a social structure became a burning issue with the impact of Women's Liberation in the 1970s.

The new feminism politicized sex role theory and generated

theories of patriarchy, and rapidly became an international movement. The United Nations, declaring 1975 International Women's Year and running world conferences through the International Decade for Women, created a very public arena for cross-cultural encounters. Feminist theory was subjected to rigorous critique from Black women within the metropole and diasporic feminists from the periphery. The result, as Chilla Bulbeck (1998) and Chandra Talpade Mohanty (2003) show, has been an intense multi-centred debate in which the concepts of gender and patriarchy have been scrutinized and the ethnocentric assumptions of much metropolitan theory laid bare.

This debate has been an uncomfortable, even painful, process. But, it is worth observing, the debate has not stopped gender analysis. As Mohanty emphasizes, it has been possible to combine a strong recognition of difference with an emphasis on solidarity and common struggle.

New lines of analysis, examining globalization as a gendered process, have been emerging. New forms of transnational feminist organizing are built around such understandings (Moghadam 2005). Gender analysis is still an intellectual force in the periphery. This was formally acknowledged by CODESRIA (Council for the Development of Social Science Research in Africa), which published *Engendering African Social Sciences* (Imam, Mama and Sow 1997). CODESRIA continues to sponsor discussions of gender research, for instance launching a Gender Series in 2004 and publishing special issues of the *CODESRIA Bulletin* on gender themes (see no. 1, 2003; no. 1/2, 2006). Gender analysis has been one of social science's main contributions to understanding and contesting the HIV/AIDS epidemic, with its devastating impact in Africa and south Asia.

Moghadam's observation about emerging responses to globalization signals an issue of general importance to sociology. Sociologists in the metropole have recognized how neoliberal market ideology undermines, or even denies, recognition of the social (Smart 2003). Since we now live in a world where neoliberal agendas frame the policies of all major states and where corporate control of the global economy has reached an unprecedented level, sociology as an intellectual project is at risk of severe marginalization. It is already marginalized in policy discourses and in mass media, compared with a generation ago. It is particularly under-represented in transnational policymaking arenas such as the OECD and the World Bank.

If this argument is broadly correct, then the 'public sociology' advocated by Michael Burawoy is not an option within the metropole, as assumed by many of Burawoy's US interlocutors (Clawson *et al.* 2007). Rather, it is a necessity on a world scale.

Neoliberal globalization itself pushes sociology into an oppositional position, since the very act of naming social structures is an obstacle to the triumph of market ideology. If sociology is not to fade into a residual science researching those who sadly fail to 'achieve' in a neoliberal world, it must connect with the energies of resistance and the intellectual critique of global domination.

Sociology, social science more generally, has something important to offer democratic movements and processes. If Comtean sociology classically embodied the colonial gaze on the colonized, contemporary sociology is in a position to gaze straight back, to articulate a democratic perspective on global power. And as Jennifer Robinson (2006) argues for urban sociology, the diverse experience and multiple social forms of the periphery are a stronger base for social science than generalization from the metropole.

To do these jobs, sociology needs to speak internationally and cross-culturally. What Martin and Beittel (1998) call a 'world-historical orientation' within a global sociological community, what Bulbeck (1998) calls a 'world-traveller perspective', are required. At such a time, debate within the metropole is not enough. Sociology from the periphery is strategic for the whole discipline, and it is essential to recognize the importance of the global periphery in the history of sociology.

8

Paulin Hountondji's Postcolonial Sociology of Knowledge

The sociology of knowledge emerged as a distinct field in the 1920s, in the work of Max Scheler (1924) and Karl Mannheim (1929) in Germany, drawing on Gyorgy Lukács (1923). It immediately aroused fierce argument. Lukács's classic *History and Class Consciousness* was denounced by his own party and repudiated by the author, soon after it was published. A few years later Mannheim's effort was also vehemently criticized, for undermining the concept of science.

The idea of a sociology of knowledge has lain around ever since in an uneasy twilight, occasionally stirring into active life – for instance when Dorothy Smith in Canada gendered it by launching *The Conceptual Practices of Power: A Feminist Sociology of Knowledge* (1990). Sociologists rather enjoy the idea that knowledge itself is socially determined. There is plenty of evidence, from studies of laboratories and other scientific institutions, that even high-prestige natural science is far from a dispassionate, socially neutral sphere. Yet natural science seems to work, in the sense that atom bombs do explode, bridges do hold up and antibiotics do (often) stop bacterial infections. And a thoroughgoing critique of science seems to undermine social science as well. So a sociology of knowledge also seems counter-intuitive or self-contradictory.

There are endless possibilities for debate here. Some have argued for a more empirical 'sociology of ideas' (Camic and Gross 2001), which avoids the paradoxes around knowledge. Yet it was precisely the critique of privileged forms of knowledge that always gave an excitement, an edge of subversiveness, to the field.

The more important problem is that the sociology of knowledge has been, from the start, deeply Eurocentric. The centrepiece of Lukács' *History and Class Consciousness* was a dazzling critique of mainstream European philosophy. Mannheim's more pedestrian *Ideology and Utopia* was equally focused on European systems of thought and political projects. Much the same has been true of later sociologists' accounts of the field. Even the feminist sociologies of knowledge have focused on European and North American patriarchy. Though we now have empirical accounts of global patterns in knowledge, the conceptual framework of the sociology of knowledge remains resolutely Northern.

This needs to change and it can. In this chapter I examine perhaps the most important contribution to this change, by a leading west African intellectual whose work addresses the making of knowledge in a postcolonial world.

A career line

Paulin J. Hountondji, born in 1942, was educated in the French-speaking schools of the colony of Dahomey (now Benin), then in an elite school in Paris, finally in the super-elite École Normale Supérieure. He was a beneficiary of the French cultural policy of selecting bright colonial youth to be trained in metropolitan institutions. He went through the classical academic curriculum, specializing in philosophy. He wound up with high honours and a PhD thesis – still unpublished – on Husserl. His well-known teachers included Derrida, Ricoeur, Canguilhem and Althusser.

Hountondji was a student in Paris through the 1960s, so witnessed the upheaval of the New Left and the May Days of 1968. Though on the left politically, he was not actively involved in the student revolt. He considered that as an African, his political responsibilities concerned Africa. He was involved in African student groups and came to know the Paris-centred network of black intellectuals that had crystallized a generation earlier in the *négritude* movement. This group still functioned as a forum for debate about black consciousness, African culture and political directions in the era of decolonization, putting out the famous journal *Présence africaine*. In was in this network, as he explains in an autobiographical book (Hountondji 2002: 79ff), that he began the work on 'African philosophy' that was to make him famous.

After teaching in a French university and completing his thesis, Hountondji returned to Africa, taking up an academic post in Zaire and experiencing first-hand the Mobutu dictatorship. In 1972 he returned to Dahomey and took up an appointment in philosophy at the National University. He was soon engaged in political struggles within the newly independent country, editing a magazine and writing the articles collected in his first book, *Libertés*.

This was published in Cotonou soon after a military coup that announced itself as establishing a revolutionary and socialist regime. Hountondji tried to spell out what would make a real revolution, emphasizing popular participation and freedom of debate and also cultural independence. In a prescient phrase, he argued for the need to 'accept the adventure of truth' and argued for basic scientific research, not just applied research, even in a very poor country (Hountondji 1973: 26, 41).

At the same time he was finishing his analysis of ethnophilosophy, published in 1976 as *Sur la 'philosophie africaine': critique de l'ethnophilosophie* (English translation *African Philosophy: Myth and Reality*, 1983). A huge controversy followed, which saw Hountondji defending and extending his argument in many forums across Africa and some in Europe.

In the 1980s he launched a reconsideration of indigenous knowledge, setting up an interdisciplinary seminar whose contributions were published, years later, as *Les savoirs endogènes: pistes pour une recherche* (*Endogenous Knowledge: Research Trails*, 1994/7). A reason why it took so long was that Hountondji was again involved in political struggle, against the increasingly dogmatic and authoritarian regime in Benin. He was active in the democratic movement of the late 1980s and was a delegate to the National Conference in 1990 that allowed a peaceful transition to democracy – one of the more successful transitions of the time.

As one of the country's leading intellectuals, Hountondji was called on to serve in the new government. He was successively Minister of Education, Minister of Culture and special advisor to the President, before leaving government in October 1994 to return to academic work. Since then he has continued to be in demand internationally as a speaker and writer. Since leaving politics he has published an intellectual autobiography and critical reflection on his own research, *Combats pour le sens* (the title is badly translated as *The Struggle for Meaning*, 2002).

African philosophy

Hountondji's reputation was established by his intervention in a debate about African culture that had been launched by Placide Tempels' *Bantu Philosophy* (1945). Tempels was a missionary, one of those who evangelized in the wake of the Belgian invasion and exploitation of central Africa – one of the most horrifying stories in the whole blood-stained history of colonial conquest. Tempels was one of a reforming, paternalist group among the colonizers, who rejected the contempt for the colonized that was so common in imperialism. His position was quite like that of Australian ethnographers of his generation, especially A. P. Elkin, also a clergyman, who defended the worth of Aboriginal cultures within a neocolonial framework.

Tempels argued that Europeans, thinking of black Africans as primitive people with primitive minds, failed to see the well-developed *implicit* philosophy that Africans already had. Tempels' central argument is that Bantu thought rests on an ontology, a theory of being, that equates being with 'vital force'. Where

Europeans see an object or a person, Africans see a force of life. These forces are in interaction with each other, usually hierarchical; thus a person lives in a community under the direction of headmen who embody a greater life-force; the living necessarily have relations with the dead (hence ancestor worship); one life-force can dominate or damage another (hence witchcraft); and so on. This ontology leads to a theory of the person, *muntu*, that is a kind of philosophical psychology; and to an ethics, that is strongly communal. All of these beliefs are based on an underlying belief in the strongest vital force of all, God.

Tempels' ethnography was, at best, amateur and his understanding of social dynamics was very limited. He was openly contemptuous of European-educated Africans – 'empty and unsatisfied souls', 'moral and intellectual tramps', 'a class of pseudo-Europeans'. Tempels did not see coming the tidal wave of decolonization that broke over Africa almost immediately, led precisely by those unsatisfied souls he despised – intellectuals like Kwame Nkrumah, who won a landslide election in what was to become Ghana, in 1951.

But Tempels wrote warmly of the coherence and profundity of African thought, 'a lofty wisdom' from which Europeans too can learn. During the two decades of anti-colonial political and cultural struggle that followed the Second World War, it was this side of Tempels' thought that had a remarkable influence. Indeed, it triggered a whole industry of research and speculation.

Tempels' amateur ethnography was soon replaced by much more sophisticated work. This began with the research of Alexis Kagamé in Rwanda, whose *Philosophie Bantu-Rwandaise de l'Être*, later turned into a broad comparative analysis (*La philosophie bantu comparée*, 1976) offered an account of indigenous ontology based on a close analysis of grammatical forms in Bantu languages. Many others contributed to the genre, and research in this tradition was still continuing forty years after Tempels began it (Gyekye 1987).

In this era of decolonization, the idea of philosophies based in indigenous cultures became a vehicle for the re-assertion of African dignity. The idea of 'African philosophy' became popular as an intellectual parallel to the literary reassertion of African consciousness and creativity in the *négritude* movement of the 1930s and 1940s. Poets such as Léopold Senghor and Aimé Césaire celebrated the experience of those who were negated, defined as Other, by white European culture. This movement became increasingly politicized as the struggles for colonial independence developed – influencing, among others, Frantz Fanon and Steve Biko.

Thus 'African philosophy' played a part in contesting the culture of imperialism and in legitimating African independence. But was it actually philosophy? By the 1960s doubts were being expressed by African intellectuals. In 1976 these doubts were crystallized by Hountondji in his brilliant and angry book *Sur la 'philosophie africaine'*.

Critique of ethnophilosophy

Hountondji was scathing about the idea of an immanent African 'philosophy' that could be discovered in customs, chants, myths and so on. He identified a deep logical confusion in the ethno-philosophers' project. Far from validating African culture, it represented an obstacle to the development of African philosophical thought.

Hountondji pointed to the lack of a clear textual base for the ethnophilosophers' interpretations and the contradictory doctrines they came up with. This 'African philosophy' was not constructed by rigorous and testable methods. It was, in fact, a loose projection of the ideas of the ethnophilosophers themselves, who

> . . . hide behind the screen, all the more opaque for being imaginary, of an implicit 'philosophy' conceived as an unthinking, spontaneous, collective system of thought, common to all Africans or at least to all members severally, past, present and future, of such-and-such an African ethnic group. (1983: 55)

As Hountondji later put it, this was an evasion of responsibility:

[Ethnophilosophers] developed a sort of philosophy in the third person, consisting of sentences like this: 'They think so and so', 'They say so and so', etc. They renounced, in a sense, speaking and arguing on their own behalf. They renounced intellectual responsibility. (1996: 83)

Further, ethnophilosophy was based on bad social analysis. It made an implausible assumption of consensus within African cultures, 'the myth of primitive unanimity, with its suggestion that in "primitive" societies – that is to say, non-Western societies – everybody always agrees with everybody else' (1983: 60). It made a false assumption that African societies were culturally static, that an unchanging world-view could be discovered in them. Far from putting authentic African philosophical work into wider circulation, ethnophilosophy reproduced the colonizers' gaze on African culture.

In short, Hountondji argued, the whole school of ethnophilosophy from Tempels onward was a 'mad and hopeless enterprise' based on 'a huge misconception' (1983: 52, 75–6) – unscientific, arbitrary and now politically reactionary. Hountondji understood that ethnophilosophy and the *négritude* movement were responses to the colonialist denigration of 'primitive' thought. But assertion of the distinctness and dignity of African culture, progressive in the time of anti-colonial struggle, changed its political colour in the neocolonial era. It now became part of the ideology of dictatorial post-independence states. Hountondji was pungent in his criticism of these regimes and their self-serving cultural orthodoxies. He had direct experience of teaching in Zaire in the time of the Mobutu dictatorship and its dogma of 'authenticity'. He now made sharp criticism of the 'complicity' between nationalists and ethnographers, the way nativist cultural theory works as an alibi for power.

Hountondji was by no means alone in questioning ethnophilosophy. For instance, the Ghanaian philosopher Kwasi Wiredu, in *Philosophy and an African Culture* (1980), made a clear distinction between 'folk thought' on the one hand and philosophy as a critical practice, based on reason and argument, on the other. But that did not save Hountondji from ferocious criticism. He was accused by the Left of being a petit-bourgeois individualist and by the right of betraying African people and culture. Ethnophilosophers saw him as committed to a Eurocentric view of philosophy. He was charged with being a neocolonialist, an elitist, a snob and an intellectual fraud. No wonder, looking back on the controversy, he called it a 'polluted debate' (Gyekye 1987; Serequeberhan 1991; Hountondji 2002: 162ff).

Yet, over time, the critique of ethnophilosophy prevailed. It did so because the critics were not abandoning issues about Africa, but thinking about them in a different way. In *African Philosophy* Hountondji also examines other ways of philosophizing, through the cases of Amo, an eighteenth-century philosopher from the Gold Coast, and Nkrumah, as a twentieth-century theorist of political development. Both Wiredu and Hountondji were centrally concerned with the *reconstruction* of African cultures and saw the question of scientific and technological knowledge as crucial.

Extroverted science

Hountondji acknowledged that one cannot simply abandon local cultural knowledge. But he insisted that ethnoscience (the academic discipline that tries to reconstruct non-Western cultures' views of plants, animals, the natural world, mathematics, etc.) represented a European gaze that defined Africans as informants, not full participants, in the making of knowledge.

African intellectuals who pursued these approaches were, as Hountondji had argued in *African Philosophy*, fundamentally adopting a European point of view. But the significance of this viewpoint *for Africans* was different. Recognition of this point led Hountondji to a key concept: 'The exclusion practiced by the European scholar becomes, when it is taken over by the African intellectual, extroversion' (Hountondji 2002: 103).

What was needed, rather than ethnoscience, was a realistic approach to local knowledges that allowed them to be seen in relation to other knowledges, criticized and reappropriated in forms that were relevant to the development of African societies. The unfolding of these views steadily moved Hountondji from conventional philosophy towards a sociology of knowledge.

The crucial step, which Hountondji seems to have made soon after writing *African Philosophy* – though the implications took a long time to work out – was to see the production of knowledge in the colony, or postcolonial country, *as part of a global political economy of knowledge*. Hountondji drew explicitly on Samir Amin's (1974) Marxist economics of accumulation on a world scale, especially Amin's analysis of the extroversion of dependent economies. He was, nevertheless, careful to avoid a simple economic reductionism. Knowledge, to Hountondji, has always been a reality in its own right.

Under colonialism, 'the integration of our subsistence economies into the world capitalist market' produced a distinctive organization of the production of knowledge:

> With respect to modern science, the heart of the process is neither the stage of data collection nor that of the application of theoretical findings to practical issues. Rather, it lies between the two, in the stages of theory building, interpretation of raw information and the theoretical processing of the data collected . . . The one essential shortcoming of scientific activity in colonial Africa was the lack of these specific theory-building procedures and infrastructures. (Hountondji 1995: 2)

In the colonies, the *theoretical* stage of science was omitted. Accordingly, the colonies became a field for the collection of raw material – scientific data – which was sent to the metropole where theory was produced. Examples of this process abound in the history of European science. Map-makers, collectors and observers travelled out to the frontiers of exploration, conquest and trade, bringing back specimens, measurements, observations and stories that were woven into European natural and social science. Key figures in the history of modern science, as important as Darwin, Banks and Humboldt, were deeply involved in this appropriation.

(I cannot resist the Australian case. As our dreadful national anthem recalls, the British colonization of the continent directly followed from a data-gathering expedition of this kind, under Captain James Cook, who 'discovered' eastern Australia, a mere 40,000 years after the Aboriginal peoples did, in 1770. We sang in school: 'When gallant Cook from Albion sailed, to trace wide oceans o'er, true British courage bore him on, till he landed on our shore; and there he raised old England's flag, the standard of the brave . . .' I have forgotten the rest.)

These colonial relationships of knowledge became increasingly institutionalized, through museums and universities in the cities of the metropole. I have already mentioned their significance for sociology, in chapter 7. They are the ancestors of the electronic databases of science today.

Hountondji further shows that this colonial structure persists powerfully in the postcolonial period. He offers various 'indices of extroversion', in an all-too-believable account of the dilemmas of intellectuals in the periphery. As he jokingly acknowledges, the list has grown over time. Here is the version in *Endogenous Knowledge* (1997: 7–12):

1. Dependence on imported apparatus, from the microscope on.
2. Dependence on journals, libraries and publishing houses in the global North; more generally, dependence on storage, preservation and dissemination of research findings in mostly Northern institutions.
3. Theoretical extroversion: the work of African scholars finds its main audience in the global North. This orientation is internalized by African researchers.
4. A resulting focus in African research on the immediate environment, local data collection, rather than 'the independent creation of theoretical models'.
5. Focusing of local research on the imperatives of an extroverted economy – e.g. the focus of agronomy on the problems of export crops, not subsistence crops.
6. The 'brain drain' to the North is only part of an orientation to the North that all Third World intellectuals are driven to – some shuttling back and forth, others looking for opportunities to migrate to the North.

7. The intellectual tourist circuit linking North and South – Third World researchers having to make the physical trip to the North to develop their careers, as a structural necessity.
8. Scientific tourism from North to South, where researchers come 'in search not of knowledge but only of materials that lead to knowledge' – information, new facts, tests for their findings.
9. Dependence of the South on metropolitan languages for scientific work, with resulting marginalization of local languages.

An example of the detail is Hountondji's discussion of scientists from the periphery trying to publish their work in metropolitan academic journals. Such journals have no expectation that theory will come from the South. Therefore:

> African scholars are often tempted, especially in the social sciences, to lock themselves up into an empirical description of the most peculiar features of their societies, without any consistent effort to interpret, elaborate on, or theorize about these features. In so doing, they implicitly agree to act as informants, though learned informants, for Western science and scientists. (Hountondji 1995: 4)

What is to be done about this? Hountondji is clear about the principle: it is a question of democratizing the global production of knowledge.

> To break that logic at last, to recover individual and collective initiative, to become ourselves again is one of the major tasks prescribed by History. That task, within the specific field of knowledge, amounts to taking an informed enough view of current practices in order to work out other possible modalities of producing knowledge, other possible forms of technological and scientific production relationships, first between the South and the North, but also in the South itself and inside each and every country. (1997: 12)

What, concretely, might those 'other possible modalities' be? Hountondji clearly thinks the reconsideration of local knowledge is part of the process.

Relativism and rationality

The main product of this argument is *Endogenous Knowledge,* published in Dakar by the Council for the Development of Social Science Research in Africa (Hountondji 1994/7). This volume, based on a seminar organized by Hountondji years before, collects studies by a variety of authors on local knowledge systems and technologies.

The scope of the collection is impressive. It includes precolonial ironworking, rainmaking, conceptual structures such as number systems and zoological names, medicine and pharmacology, and forms of transmission of knowledge, graphic, written and oral.

On the one hand, these can be seen as separate and autonomous knowledge systems, to be studied by historical and ethnographic methods. Around the time this book was being put together, Hountondji (1990) explicitly argued for a sociology of 'collective representations', adopting a familiar terminology from French social science. An epistemological pluralism, a radical cultural relativism, could follow.

But the task of intellectuals in Africa is not just the development of contemplative science; it is to put knowledge to work in addressing severe practical problems. Not accidentally, this was the time when Hountondji became a Minister of Education and a Minister of Culture in Benin. A radical pluralism was not a practical proposition. *Endogenous Knowledge* thus addresses the *relation* between local knowledge and metropolitan science. It is not only a matter of documenting the wealth of local knowledges:

> There is a further need to learn to *scrutinize* them in order to extract the essential kernel, to *purify* them by separating the myth in which they are wrapped up, just as right here in Africa, metals used to be separated from mineral ores. Finally, one must learn to re-integrate such forms of knowledge thus reclaimed into the movement of living science, into the new dynamics that carries us nowadays forward, us and our societies. (1997: 35–6)

The segregation between Western science and local knowledges can thus be broken down by a rational critique. This is the path to the democratic goal, 'to demarginalize Africa and the Third World with regard to knowledge as well as in all other respects' (1997: 36). Hountondji thus comes to the dilemma about relativism that is faced by every sociology of knowledge. He solves the problem by making 'a wager for rationality' (2002: 254), that is, a common rationality, for essentially practical and democratic reasons. He is certainly aware of the arguments for multiple knowledge systems, indeed has recently edited a volume posing the question *La rationalité, une ou plurielle?* (*Rationality, single or plural?* Hountondji 2007). His own view is clearly that there must be a common rationality, because of the fact of communication between cultures.

What troubles him is not so much the impossibility of communication, as practical confusion in the relation between knowledge systems. In more than one text he gives the example of the Western-educated doctor in Africa who, unable to cure a disorder, sends the patient off to a traditional healer. And he knows about the appropriation of traditional herbal lore by transnational pharmaceutical corporations. In his reflection on educational problems, he argued for building up technical education in Third-World countries, to make post-school education locally relevant rather than producing generations of unemployable university graduates (Hountondji, Mudimbe and Appiah 1991). There is a certain tension between that argument and his earlier defence of fundamental-science research in poor postcolonial countries.

Reflections

Hountondji's work has important implications for understanding the problems of intellectual work and intellectual workers far beyond west Africa. Australia, for instance, is by no means a Third World country. It has a small rich capitalist economy and an affluent standard of living. But it is a peripheral country, which has a marginal position in the global structure of knowledge production, as it does in the economy of goods and services. Most fields of intellectual work in Australia are 'extroverted' in Hountondji's sense. Biographically, as our life-history and survey data show, Australian intellectual workers face a centre/margin problem and have an orientation to the global metropole, rather than to the world as a whole (see chapter 6).

Hountondji's analysis of the global structuring of knowledge production works at three levels: (a) the practices of individual researchers, (b) the functioning of institutions and (c) epistemology.

In relation to individual researchers, Hountondji offers sardonic but very perceptive comments on the intellectual tourist circuit and the career dilemmas of researchers in the periphery. They are tied together by a reproductionist argument – the practices that emerge as responses to these problems tend to reproduce the subordination of the periphery. Yet Hountondji is not a reproductionist in the manner of Bourdieu's *Homo Academicus*. Hountondji emphasizes, in *African Philosophy* and *The Struggle for Meaning*, the personal responsibility of intellectuals for the stances they take and the statements they make. This strongly implies a capacity for independent action, which is richly illustrated by Hountondji's own career. His discussion of ethnophilosophy clearly implies that intellectuals in the postcolonial world can make *strategic* choices, can act differently to good effect. *Endogenous Knowledge* is the proof.

In relation to institutions, Hountondji draws on historical work about the functioning of museums and universities, but also on contemporary experience of knowledge institutions such as journals, databanks and publishing houses. This level of his argument is the least developed. I think his insights are broadly correct and point to a rich field for research on the structures of the international circulation of knowledge.

Being a professional philosopher, Hountondji is most at home at the epistemological level. Here his argument implies a powerful revision of the classical sociology of knowledge. Hountondji's work makes a metropole-centric perspective no longer credible. Drawing on Althusser's most creative work – his analysis of ideology and science – Hountondji shows the colonial and neocolonial division of labour at the heart of modern science, the concentration of theoretical work in the global metropole and the enormous difficulty of autonomous theoretical development in the periphery. We can now understand the appeal of ethnophilosophy as a solution to this dilemma (and it is interesting that in retrospect, Hountondji (2002) has taken a gentler view of its practitioners), while still recognizing it as a pseudo-science.

The problem of the autonomy of the periphery was addressed in sociology by the 'indigenous sociology' movement of the 1980s and 1990s (e.g. Akiwowo 1986, 1999). This movement tried to find in pre-colonial oral culture elements of social knowledge that could be extracted and re-combined into an alternative theoretical framework for sociology. Hountondji's profound critique of ethnophilosophy immediately applies to this conception of indigenous sociology.

Yet Hountondji's later work opens up a more positive line of thought. Local knowledge is, indeed, of great importance to development. But to make use of it, Hountondji argues, we must be concerned with the *truth* of indigenous knowledge, the reasons for its effectiveness, as well as critically examining the reasons it was bound up with myth and magic and the misuses of indigenous knowledge by contemporary myth-makers.

I think this argument applies forcibly to the social sciences. The *knowledge of social situations* embedded in indigenous discourses about society is knowledge of the same order – as detailed, subtle, grounded in experience and contestable – as metropolitan discourses about metropolitan society. Moving from the informal knowledge of social situations to the formal discourse of social science has to happen in both cases, and in both cases there must be a process of critique that establishes relations between local and generalizable knowledge.

A crucial fact is that colonialism itself changes the terms on which this can be done. Contemporary knowledge is post-colonial, not just as a matter of dating but because the social situations it addresses are those created by the history of imperialism and globalization. In a colony of settlement such as Australia, the structure of 'local knowledge' is profoundly complex, since indigenous knowledge is overlaid by the cultures of successive immigrant populations, which in turn form dynamic hierarchies. This assemblage is constantly transformed by pressures from the global metropole. There is constant re-working of the terms in which local experience is articulated.

The processes of producing knowledge in the metropole and the periphery and in rich and poor countries of the periphery, are differently structured *in practice*. This follows from the global inequalities, the legacy of imperialism, that have constituted the metropole as the home of theory, or 'science' as such, and the periphery as either the source of data, or the arena in which metropolitan knowledge is applied.

The dilemma that Hountondji faces and in my view never quite resolves, is about the status of 'universal' knowledge or common rationality. Hountondji drew from his study of Husserl, and his work with teachers such as Althusser, a conviction of the inner rationality of science. Hountondji's is an attractive position, if now sociologically unfashionable, because it grounds critique of local ideological systems and provides a rationale for the appropriation of 'Western' knowledge in the education systems of developing countries. But it ignores the critique of scientific rationality that has been developed by feminist science studies in the metropole (Crowley and Himmelweit 1992) and the question of alternative foundations for science and technology that has been raised in Islamic discussions of knowledge (Ghamari-Tabrizi 1996). I think that Hountondji's position on this issue will need repair.

But it does lead to one conclusion that gives me pause, because it is undoubtedly correct for the social sciences. Reflecting on metropolitan debates about science, Hountondji acknowledged the point made by Kuhn, among others, that a kind of conformity made science in the industrialized countries work.

> But I also found out that this same conformity, transposed to the Third World, would be a disaster. The researcher at the periphery had to be more critical, more demanding and more radical. Rather than these 'cleaning-up' operations that characterized 'normal science' in the Center and that aim essentially at fitting facts to paradigms, the

researcher in the periphery has to go back to the paradigms themselves, to interrogate them and, if necessary, to challenge them. (Hountondji 2002: 241)

It is hard to think of a better argument for southern theory! We are indebted to Hountondji for the first really powerful general analysis of the working of Eurocentric knowledge production in the global periphery. The sociology of knowledge should never be the same again.

9

Antonio Negri's Theory of Empire

Antonio Negri, philosopher, activist and architect of class struggle, was perhaps the most brilliant theorist in the New Left of the 1960s and 1970s. He is now, on the strength of books published since he turned sixty, one of the most influential analysts of global power. Negri has produced work of tremendous scope. He has a truly impressive capacity for synthesis, for finding deep patterns that link disparate issues. I think he makes some false moves and leaves large gaps in his picture of the world. Yet his work throws off sparks in all directions. In this chapter I explore his theory of global Empire and its roots in his earlier thinking and political experience.

The picture of Empire

In a long essay on materialism written in the late 1990s (Negri 2003) and in two sprawling books written with the US literary theorist Michael Hardt, *Empire* (2000) and *Multitude* (2004), Negri sets out a distinctive analysis of power and struggle in global society. (Hardt undoubtedly played a large part in producing these texts and expanding Negri's knowledge of US politics, history and intellectual life. Nevertheless it is clear that the basic analysis is Negri's.)

Negri pictures a power structure that operates on a world scale. The accumulation of power is greater than it has ever been, yet sovereignty has been dispersed. Modern capitalism has produced a strange political order, quite different from the colonialism of the nineteenth century. There are levels in this power structure and 'apexes and summits of imperial power' (Hardt and Negri 2000: 355) – particularly the US state and its nuclear armaments. Yet this eminence does not give the US government the capacity to administer the world. Sovereign power is widely dispersed in network fashion. The strongest centres can, at best, conduct police operations and they need help from other parts of the network.

At the same time Empire has become, in a certain sense, total. There is no 'outside' to the system. For instance there is no transcendent ethical standpoint from which its operations can be effectively criticized.

There are echoes of Foucault here, but Negri's model is very different from one of 'capillary' power. The dispersed sovereignty of Empire is still a system of domination, specifically, capitalist domination: 'in Empire capital and sovereignty tend to overlap completely' (Hardt and Negri 2004: 334). It is a system designed to maintain exploitation and the accumulation of wealth in the hands of the privileged few.

Such a system has to be violent, hard-headed and ruthless. *Empire* was published before the 9/11 atrocity, but the model has no difficulty accounting for the US response to the attack and for the subsequent atrocities against Afghanistan and Iraq. *Multitude* argues that war, the extreme expression of the violence of the system, has become endemic and indeed necessary to the global order: 'military force must guarantee the conditions for the functioning of the world market' (Hardt and Negri 2004: 21, 90, 177).

Empire is a system of domination produced by rupture from earlier systems of domination. The new society is marked by hybrid forms of rule, cobbled together to deal ad hoc with urgent

problems. Examples are private police, 'public-private partnerships', puppet governments. There is no orderliness in the global
exercise of power. But there is an overall character to it:

> In Empire corruption is everywhere . . . It resides in different forms
> in the supreme government of Empire and its vassal administrations,
> the most refined and the most rotten administrative police forces, the
> lobbies of the ruling classes, the mafias of rising social groups . . .
> the great financial conglomerates and everyday economic transac-
> tions. Through corruption, imperial power extends a smoke screen
> across the world and command over the multitude is exercised in
> this putrid cloud, in the absence of light and truth. (Hardt and Negri
> 2000: 389)

Empire is a new form of the state; but it is a state that has achieved
an eerie autonomy from society. Negri suggests that the mediations
are dying, that civil society – far from flourishing, as optimistic globalization theorists like Beck (1999) and Giddens (2002) think – is
withering away. The established institutions of modern society,
such as school, family, hospital, factory, 'are everywhere in crisis'
(Hardt and Negri 2000: 329). In their place arises a society of
control. Negri has no patience with social-democratic wailing
about the decline of the state under globalization. In his view, big
government has never gone away. It has, however, changed its
focus – from economic planning to social control, the mobilization
of force, 'security'.

As a good Marxist, Negri sees an economic rationale in this
political order. Empire is capitalist power being exerted over a
new system of production. Adapting language from Foucault,
Negri speaks of 'biopolitical production', meaning that capitalist
exploitation has stretched its scope, from the simple making of
commodities in the traditional factory, to the making of the whole
pattern of life.

'Immaterial production', involving new forms of labour centring on the exchange of information and on human emotion, is
now hegemonic. Here Negri draws on recent discussions of com-
puterization, the 'information society', the service economy and

emotion work. The 'commons' produced by the new groups of workers are now the targets of capitalist expropriation.

Almost alone among theorists of globalization, Negri does not see the creation of global society as a process driven from the top. Exactly the opposite. He argues that the new forms of rule, and of global economic organization, are *reactive*. They are the responses of capital to pressure from below. There is no other way it could be, because capital is not in itself creative.

Negri goes to some length, in his philosophical work, to emphasize the unique creativity of *labour*, 'the power to create being where there is only the void' (Negri 2003: 242). In bio-political production, this creativity can be seen across the whole terrain of human life. In earlier phases, the capitalist did hands-on organizing of some of this labour (the iron master in his factory). Now, capital simply exercises control from a distance (the billion-aire at Palm Beach). Capital has become wholly parasitical on the creativity of its labour force.

But the labour force – which in biopolitical production is very extensive and diverse – is not passive. Rather it is a seething mass of resistance to the control that capital attempts to exert. The resistance takes a tremendous variety of forms. Negri mentions some examples of resistance, from workplace struggles to anticolonial wars to uncontrolled labour migration. He notes both continuity with earlier forms of working-class struggle and new figures of resistance such as the Zapatistas. Empire does its best to pathologize and police them all. Resistance is necessarily lived as otherness, as the *refusal* of capitalist social relations and the creation of other ways of life.

Here, Negri speaks of the 'self-valorization' involved in prole-tarian struggle. By this he means the creation of a life fundamentally *separate* from the set of social relations that capital attempts to impose. Negri thus argues that we are living in a society not tending to polarize (as in old Marxist models) but *already* dichoto-mous, in its basic processes. The global capitalist state and the capitalist corporations sit on top of a population which is always escaping their control, always creating new forms of life, and which basically does not need them.

In his recent books, Negri adopts a modified 'postmodernity' thesis and argues that the old class structure and the old class dynamics have gone. The dialectic has been broken. And with it, into the dustbin of history go all the strategies that ever tried to unify the proletariat around the industrial worker or the militant peasant, or under the leadership of a vanguard party.

Instead of growing unity of the working class, Negri sees irreducible diversity. Here he is strongly influenced by Deleuze and Guattari's *A Thousand Plateaus*. 'The postmodern multitude is an ensemble of singularities' (Negri 2003: 225). Rather than seeing diversity as an obstacle to class mobilization, Negri sees it as the very tissue of resistance, something to celebrate, a feature of democratic action in the postmodern world.

'Multitude' in Negri's usage is not a sociological term; he is not offering it as the name for a new transnational working class. 'Multitude' is a concept referring to a new *composition* of the proletariat, a new pattern of resistance to capital, a new configuration of social struggles. The crucial point is an absolute separation from capital:

> . . . within the context of the sovereign organization of globality, Empire is directly confronted by the multitude and the multitude by Empire. In this context, all mediations tend to disintegrate. (Negri 2003: 229)

There is no vanguard group, no master strategy and there cannot possibly be one. Rather, there is a tremendous many-sided outpouring of creativity and resistance around the world. The resistance of the multitude is uncontrollable partly because it is shapeless. There is no world revolutionary HQ that the Pentagon can bomb. More fundamentally, the multitude is uncontrollable because resistance is inherent in the creativity of living labour. Since capital absolutely depends on living labour, it can never get rid of the resistance and it cannot overcome the separation. That is the contradiction in which Empire finds itself and which will ultimately destroy it.

Within the resistance, Negri finds the outline of something

that can replace Empire, indeed capitalism itself. Creative labour, especially the new patterns of biopolitical labour based on intellect and emotion, construct forms of social solidarity and decision-making among the proletariat. The emerging forms of life that are the process of self-valorization constitute commons that are inherently, directly, democratic. In the capacity of the multitude to create new democratic forms of life, Negri finds the basis of a *constituent power* that contests Empire. This constituent power is capable of taking the revolutionary leap beyond capitalism into a world of cooperative labour and universal freedom.

This will not, however, be achieved by sweetness and light. Capitalist power opposes all these processes with violence. Therefore the movements of resistance and transformation must be prepared to use force themselves – as, indeed, many of them do. The process is a social revolution.

There are other themes in *Empire, Multitude* and *Time for Revolution*. These books are peppered with entertaining and annoying side-essays on a wild array of topics, from vampires and insect swarms to Dostoyevsky and Machiavelli. However the points just outlined are, I think, the core of Negri's theory of contemporary society. This is perhaps the most dynamic theory of globalization we currently have and the most optimistic – despite its black picture of exploitation, violence and corruption.

The revolutionist's element

I now want to consider the background of these ideas in Negri's life, especially in his earlier theorizing. Negri came of age in an Italy dominated by conservative, corrupt Christian Democrat governments that were cold-war allies of the USA and internal allies of the church, the mafia and big capital. The main left-wing alternative was the Communist Party (PCI). This party had called off the social revolution underway in Italy at the end of the war and settled down to life as a loyal opposition. Meanwhile, the Marshall

Plan triggered a very rapid export-led industrialization, mainly in the northern cities. Italian GNP grew at more than 5 per cent per annum through the 1950s, one of the fastest growth rates in the world. Huge internal migration created new labour forces exposed for the first time to factory discipline, and began to overwhelm urban services, housing and social welfare in cities such as Turin, Milan, Rome and in the Veneto region. The result was growing social turbulence which erupted in mass protests through the 1960s (Ginsborg 1990).

Negri trained in philosophy and law and launched a stellar academic career, becoming a professor of law in his home town Padua in 1959. In the early 1960s he connected with other Marxist intellectuals who were looking for a more radical path than the PCI offered. The most influential was Mario Tronti, whose 1966 book *Operai e capitale* (workers and capital) is a foundational statement for a whole European movement to re-value working-class experience and activism. With Tronti and others, Negri edited the influential journal *Quaderni rossi* (red notebooks) and then *Classe operaia* (working class). He became a central figure in the group *Potere operaio* (workers' power), which emphasized factory-based mass action for social goals. Important gains in wages and conditions for the new industrial workers were won by direct action.

But the New Left could not hold together. Some thought the new militancy could transform the mass parties (Tronti, among others, joined the PCI). Others thought the movement should evolve into an insurrectionary vanguard party. *Potere operaio* split over this issue and collapsed in 1973, amid a widespread fragmentation of the Left. From the fragments emerged small urban guerrilla groups who regarded themselves as an armed vanguard. In the course of the 1970s they moved from defending against police and neofascists, to an aggressive campaign of violence against government officials, factory managers and prominent capitalists. The most important groups were known as *Brigate rosse* (red brigades). Meanwhile the PCI moved the other way, invented the 'Eurocommunist' strategy and sought a deal with the Christian Democrats. Negri subjected this 'historic compromise' strategy to withering criticism in a short book *Proletari e stato* (proletarians and the State, 1976).

Negri stuck with the model of decentralized mass action, which crystallized in the mid 1970s as the *Autonomia operaia* (workers' autonomy) or *Autonomia organizzata* (organized autonomy) movement. His theoretical work now emphasized links between the factory and new social movements. Again his position was vindicated. Renewed factory activism, a youth movement, a student movement, free radio, housing occupations, the new feminism, all seemed to follow a strategy of direct action to create a liberated way of life outside mainstream institutions.

In 1977 these movements erupted in another tremendous surge of social protest. Negri had his first experience of arrest and exile. In the same year his theoretical masterpiece, *La forma stato* (the state-form), was released by the radical publisher Feltrinelli. In January 1978 Feltrinelli published Negri's most apocalyptic work, *Il dominio e il sabotaggio* (domination and sabotage). Both books predicted growing class antagonism and the overthrow of the system. The final chapter of *Il dominio e il sabotaggio* is titled '. . . and the proletarians attack heaven'.

By this time the Italian political establishment was more than alarmed. The red brigades, in March 1978, kidnapped and later killed the Christian Democrat leader Aldo Moro – a story told by the great novelist Leonardo Sciascia (1978) in one of the most remarkable pieces of political writing I know. The regime opted for repression. In April 1979 the leading figures of the *Autonomia* network, and others who had been in *Potere operaio*, were gaoled. More arrests followed, continuing into 1980; the police net eventually caught about 3000 left activists. The red brigades were destroyed; but so was the core of the Italian extraparliamentary opposition.

Negri was accused by the media of being 'the brain behind the red brigades', an 'evil teacher' corrupting youth, and was actually accused of the Moro murder as well as other crimes of violence. All charges of violence against Negri were eventually dropped for lack of evidence, but the prosecutors substituted charges of incitement to insurrection mainly based on his writings. I have read part of the transcript of Negri's interrogation and it is obvious that judge and prosecutor were on a fishing expedition. On these charges Negri was eventually convicted and sentenced to thirty years imprisonment – but by then he wasn't there.

In a startling turn, in 1983 Negri was nominated for parliament by the Radical Party, a small-'l' liberal group dismayed by the state's attack on civil liberties, and was elected. This got him out of prison, because Italian MPs were immune from prosecution. But when the parliament voted to strip Negri of his immunity and send him back to prison, he very reasonably feared for his life and fled the country.

For the next fourteen years Negri lived in France. He worked as an academic, keeping a low profile politically because of his insecure residence rights as a refugee. Successive French governments, to their credit, refused to extradite him to Italy. Successive Italian governments refused an amnesty. In 1997, at the age of sixty-four, Negri returned to Italy, still facing a prison sentence (though the outrageous original sentence had been sharply reduced on appeal). It seems he hoped to broker an amnesty for militants who were still in gaol, but the deal fell through. He was sent back to prison and was still there when *Empire* was published in the USA by that well-known leftist firm, Harvard University Press, and made him world-famous.

Negri served out his term, being finally released in 2003. Since then he has travelled, written and taught again in Paris. G. B. Shaw once observed that the proper element for a revolutionist is hot water. I think Antonio Negri qualifies.

State power, the working class and sabotage

Negri's intellectual work started with a commitment to Marxism, but also to a re-reading of Marx. This reading rejected the mechanical sociology of 'historical materialism' (base, superstructure, modes of production, etc.) and saw Marxism as above all a theory of social struggle. By the mid 1970s Negri was arguing that the workers' struggle itself had made some of Marx's basic concepts obsolete.

Negri's first distinctive contribution was analysis of the Keynesian state. In a brilliant essay of 1967 Negri showed how the growth of working-class power in Europe drove the development of Keynes' economic thought and even shaped the fundamental ideas of the *General Theory*. In the following years Negri traced the development of the Keynesian 'planning-state' (*Stato-piano*) as a capitalist response to working-class pressure. He then, in a key text called *Crisi dello Stato-piano* (crisis of the planning-state, 1974a), diagnosed the disruption of the planning-state and the emergence of a 'crisis-state' or 'enterprise-state'.

Why does the capitalist state mutate? Basically, Negri argues, because working-class struggle damages the underlying *economic* mechanisms of the capitalist system. Negri puts this in Marxist language by saying that working-class struggle destroys the 'law of value' that governs exchange in the labour market, and tends to disrupt all the mechanisms of the circulation of capital. Therefore the capitalist economy cannot work as an automatic, self-regulating system. Capitalism is, in another characteristic phrase of Negri's, de-structured or de-composed by struggle.

Capital responds by an extension of state power, which – through planning – apparently restores market relations. That is widely recognized. Where Negri differs from conventional theories is his insistence that this solution is extremely unstable. With the law of value in tatters, there is no *rational* basis for any distribution of income that the state decrees. The exercise of state power becomes fundamentally arbitrary. In Negri's language, the planning-state increasingly becomes a system of contentless command. Its function now is essentially a police function; it loses legitimacy and lurches into crisis.

Therefore capital is forced to try another tack. The pressure can only be relieved 'within a project that is qualitatively differ-ent from that of reformist planning' (Red Notes 1979: 34). This new political project involves the separation of production from circulation, the creation of a 'productive subject' who does not act collectively, a new capitalist strategy for the labour market and globalization. Negri is, here, analysing the strategy of neoliberalism in response to the crisis of the Keynesian welfare state. (It is worth saying that the texts where Negri first made this analysis were written in 1973, long before Thatcher or Reagan came to power.)

At the same time, capital is forced to extend the technique of factory control to the whole of society. Civil society dies and with it all possibility of Gramscian hegemony. In a startling reversal, 'to the state, accumulation; to the enterprise, legitimation, the carrying of consensus' (Negri 1977: 245). Productivity becomes the only basis of legitimacy. Meanwhile the state, as a system of contentless command, relies more and more heavily on the use of force. In enforcing capitalist command,

> . . . administrative rationality does not become terror, it is terror. Remove from capitalist society its only rationality, which is grounded in the lust for exploitation: you have this baroque monster of provocation and devastation. (Negri 1977: 259)

Disrupting proletarian movements, establishing total control and enforcing the norms of business – 'this is "good government" today' (Negri 1977: 248). Negri and his colleagues may have been taken tactically unaware by the 1979 crackdown, but conceptually he did predict what good government in the Italian style was about to do.

All these developments come about because of pressure from the working class. The *Quaderni rossi* group emphasized the generative power of the working class and developed the concept of the changing 'class composition' of the proletariat. Negri developed these ideas into a dramatic theory of class transformations. Classical socialism had been based on a working class where the central role was played by professionalized workers (we would say 'skilled trades'). During the twentieth century, industry was transformed and the central place was taken by the 'mass worker' of the new industrial economy. While traditional communist and socialist parties watched uncomprehendingly, entirely new forms of revolutionary struggle emerged, centred in the factories. It was this challenge that disrupted the planning-state and forced capitalism down a new path.

The new path involved a second transformation of the working class. Through the 1970s Negri increasingly emphasized that contemporary capital depended on exploiting social production as a whole. This implied the growing economic importance of workers beyond the big factories – 'the social majority of the working class', including those involved in domestic labour and service work. Militancy and direct action were now emerging on this new terrain and the working class was being re-composed. New demands became politically central, especially those concerned with the social wage, that is, public sector spending.

This might sound like a recipe for compromise. But in Negri's eyes the re-composed working class was no less militant than the mass worker and no more integrated into capitalism. A new theory of working-class struggle was needed. In a long essay called with marked irony 'The workers' party against work', Negri (1974b) argued that a new phase of class conflict has emerged. Where previous forms of socialism had valorized work (think trade union banners, the 'dignity of labour'), modern proletarian struggle centres on the *refusal of work* and the disruption of capitalist command (for instance in factory occupations). In later writings Negri added an emphasis on the direct appropriation of the products of labour (e.g. housing occupations, free public transport, production for social needs).

'Autonomy' was a word with multiple meanings at the time, but it did capture this idea of ongoing *separation* from the capitalist system. Here Negri was furthest from new-left theorizing in other countries, which tended to emphasize the *integration* of the working class in advanced capitalism. (I have to declare an interest, as I was one of the people who thought that way – Connell 1977: ch. 10.)

Negri drew these threads together in the concept of 'self-valorization' (*autovalorizzazione*). With the disruption of the capitalist circuits that define the value of labour-power, it was open to the working class to give their own value to their own labour. They could turn their energy to the reproduction of their own lives. Negri saw this as the common theme in all the social struggles that had emerged from 1968 on. He therefore interpreted self-valorization as implying the immediate realization of 'communism', the new society where labour was at last free.

Here was no laborious Marxist scheme of transition between modes of production and no role for an orthodox party. The militant working class was in effect its own party, and communism was an 'active force' here and now, not pie in the sky. Negri's argument immediately linked the process of self-valorization and political organization for revolution. Translated to the language of the US New Left, his theory said: 'Do it!'

But every step of self-valorization was at the same time a step in the de-structuring of capital. Therefore, as Negri eventually put it, every form of struggle constituted *sabotage* of the system. The stories of the capitalist class and the working class were linked, but not in a dialectic. They were linked by an irreconcilable antagonism resulting in a growing separation. Only one course for working-class militancy was now open: a leap into the future, 'the proletarians attack heaven'. In a context of widening social struggle, Negri saw power shifting towards the working class, with an immediate possibility of social revolution.

Negri's writings could readily be interpreted as incitement to insurrection, because that is exactly what they were – in the context of a social revolution. They were not an incitement to terrorism.

There is no ambiguity about this point. Negri was profoundly critical of the groups who conducted the terror campaign. Negri has never been a pacifist and in the 1970s went further than supporting self-defence. He expounded the need for armed struggle in the context of mass actions confronting a violent state and capitalist command in the enterprise. It was entirely consistent with this view to reject the strategy of terrorism, pursued by groups that were trying to substitute themselves for the working class and operate as a clandestine elite (see e.g. Negri 1974b). This was not just a tactical criticism of the red brigades. The main lines of Negri's theorizing completely contradicted their strategy. The prosecutors were not interested in such subtlety and nailed him just the same.

Lines of critique

It will be clear that some of the most creative ideas in Negri's analysis of contemporary global power come from his earlier theorizing. Some of the difficulties in *Empire* and *Multitude* also have deep roots. The first problem is Negri's masculinism. His theorizing certainly breaks with orthodox Marxism. But it never breaks from the heavy-masculine style of militancy and theory that orthodox Marxism shared. Negri's writing in both periods is declamatory, accusatory and dogmatic in style.

The tough male factory worker is the implicit hero of all the 'workers' power' theorizing and it is not surprising in gender terms that this movement produced violence. Similar figures of militancy, waving clenched fists, seem to stand on all the thousand plateaus among the multitude. Negri's 1981 monograph 'The constitution of time', and the joint book *Labor of Dionysus*, mount bitter attacks on the idea of peace and the practice of nonviolence. These passages seem to me the most intemperate and ill-judged that Negri ever wrote.

Negri as a theorist pays little attention to gender, generation or sexuality. The working class and the multitude notionally include women, but not substantively, and don't seem to include children at all. In *Crisi dello Stato-piano* there is an amazing attack on the idea that radicals can have fun while they subvert the system! Grim struggle and hatred of the class enemy are the order of the day.

The masculine hardness of Negri's stances sometimes gives his writing great rhetorical power. I am haunted by his evocation of the trajectories of capitalist power and proletarian resistance/ constituent power under the shadow of nuclear catastrophe:

> These two lines move on the horizon of the world as an ungraspable alterity. (Hardt and Negri 1994: 312)

But this quality also undermines his political judgements. Negri had good reason for rejecting the PCI. But when he theorized social democracy as the agent of the terroristic strategy of the multinational corporations, he passed all limits of credibility ('Theses on the Crisis', in Negri 1974b). Similarly in *Empire* and *Multitude* Negri can see no virtue in working within institutions such as the United Nations. He can see little value in NGOs, which 'cannot change the system that produces and reproduces poverty' (Hardt and Negri 2004: 279). The only virtue seems to be in separation and biopolitical resistance. At the least, Negri's attitude involves a startling waste of political experience around the world.

A second deeply problematic feature of Negri's thought is its Eurocentrism. This was perhaps understandable in the heat of industrial battles in northern Italy. In a contemporary theorist of globalization, it is much more worrying. Negri's intellectual sources are almost all European and the few exceptions are North Americans.

Negri shows little familiarity with, and no curiosity about, non-Western intellectuals, concepts and debates. I haven't found a single reference to Muslim intellectual debates in *Empire* or *Multitude* – and Islam has a 150–year tradition of debate about capitalist global power! (See e.g. Vahdat 2002.) These two books make gestures towards other parts of the world, for instance citing the Zapatistas and the ANC as agents of struggle. But Negri never discusses *substantively* social structures or social struggles in the majority world. I think he simply doesn't know much about the world beyond Europe and hasn't thought it necessary to find out.

As a result, Negri can't see anything specific in the relationship of metropole to periphery. Indeed he specifically rejects ideas that emphasize this relationship, such as underdevelopment theory or the world-systems approach. In the typical fashion of metropolitan social theorists – left, right or centre – Negri imposes a *homogeneous* model of power on the world, insisting that Empire is much the same everywhere.

A third problem in his theorizing provides a partial explanation. Negri offers a social theory without a substantive sociology. This was already an issue in his earlier writing, which was strong on abstracted 'tendencies' but weak on descriptive detail. He didn't ask *how widely* the tendencies were present, *how much* self-valorization was happening, and what *other* social processes were also happening on the same terrain. And without hard information on these questions, Negri's belief that capitalism had entered a time of revolutionary crisis – an assumption underpinning all his work in the 1970s – remained a hopeful guess.

At least his theorizing at that period *was* based on years of personal involvement in actual industrial struggles, especially in the Veneto. There is no such practical knowledge underpinning *Empire* and *Multitude*.

The lack of concrete knowledge is strikingly revealed in the account of power. *Empire* presents a theory of global capitalism in crisis but never discusses actual multinational corporations, their strategies or problems. Negri discusses theories of sovereignty at great length but never analyses particular regimes. He conceptualizes worldwide sovereignty but never explores who is actually deploying it, how these people coordinate economic policies and military interventions, precisely what opposition they run into, nor what conflicts of interest and differences of strategy are found among them. 'Power', in short, remains an abstract postulate not a sociological reality.

The 'multitude' is even vaguer as a social entity. After following the concept through three books, I – and, I think, any reader – would be hard put to say exactly who is part of the multitude and who is not, and just how its composition is changing and why. Negri, perhaps as a result of collaborating with a literary theorist, increasingly talks about a 'figure' of resistance rather than a *group* engaged in historically located practices.

Without the sociology, the drama of self-valorization and the principle of dynamic separation – the basic ideas carried forward from the days of *Potere operaio* and *Autonomia* that underpin the concept of the Multitude and predict the overthrow of Empire – cannot become a credible model of change. The theorizing of 1998, like the theorizing of 1978, has an apocalyptic edge, but the apocalypse isn't happening at any particular address.

What Negri has given us

Though Negri's theorizing does not, in my view, provide a credible picture of world capitalism or the dynamics of change, I still
think that analysts and activists can learn a lot from it. Even his
flawed account of Empire has valuable insights into globalization.
Negri emphasizes that global capitalism is an unstable and dynamic
improvisation, not a well-entrenched, automatically functioning system. Global capitalism is the child of crisis tendencies and
it contains ongoing contradictions. Well, other people have said
that. What Negri uniquely emphasizes is that the global system has
been improvised in response to pressure *from below*, the de-structuring pressure of the exploited, and that it continues to evolve in
response to challenge and resistance from below.

Across his career Negri has given us notable insights into the
modern state. Back in the 1970s, his work was streets ahead of the
dreary instrumentalist-vs-structuralist debate about the capitalist
state, in understanding the changing form of the state, the twists
and turns of economic strategy, and the potential for violence in
advanced capitalism. His 1990s model of Empire is far too abstract,
but there is something right in his argument about network power
and about the limited capacities of particular power centres, even
the government of the sole superpower.

In his earlier work Negri made an astonishing prediction of
neoliberalism, now the dominant political framework of our
world. He shows its roots not in economic truth but in the failure
of previous capitalist strategies. He recognizes its search for total-
ity and its capacity for violence. He diagnoses the purposelessness
and sterility of the neoliberal order, the fundamental arbitrariness
of its techniques of rule, and the pervasive corruption that comes
with it.

Negri gives a central place in social dynamics to *labour* – a
concept that contemporary social theory and philosophy have
practically forgotten. In his early work Negri gave an insightful
account of labour and its social embodiment, including the changing composition of the working class. This is carried forward,

with different terminology, in his recent discussions of 'immaterial labour'.

Most suggestive of all is Negri's continuing emphasis on the creativity of labour, its unique capacity to make worlds. The concept of self-valorization ties this emphasis on creativity to a streak of eschatology in Negri's social thought. But even without the expectation that a communist utopia may arrive next Tuesday, the idea of self-valorization raises very interesting questions about labour processes, the limits of control in advanced capitalism and – I have to say it – working-class autonomy.

Finally, Negri gives us one of the most striking examples in our generation of the engaged intellectual. There is something to learn here about both endurance and willingness to learn. Under conditions of great stress Negri has produced a life-long stream of original ideas and writing. Despite appalling setbacks he has kept a deep optimism about the possibilities of social change and grassroots activism. Whether we agree with his arguments or not, we can honour someone who has never given up on the cause of human emancipation.

10

Bread and Waratahs: A Letter to the Next Left

This essay was written for the literary magazine *Overland*, as part of a series leading up to its 200th issue. It is partly autobiographical; I have been involved with Australian radical politics since the 1960s. The essay is local in detail. (A waratah, by the way, is a beautiful red flower on a dark-leaved small tree, the state symbol of New South Wales. This is my riff on the socialist–feminist phrase 'bread and roses'.) Yet Australian politics is closely tied to global social dynamics. I think the story told and the questions raised are relevant more widely.

Looking backward

When *Overland*'s first issue was printed in 1954, the Left in Australia was fairly easy to define. The Left consisted of a large, blokey faction in the Labor Party and the unions, plus a fast-shrinking Communist Party, plus a small crowd of intellectuals and peace marchers orbiting around those organizations. Everyone in this orbit assumed that working-class militancy was the great engine of change and a worker's republic was the goal. When I joined the Labor Party in 1966, my membership ticket had printed on it the famous Socialization Objective, committing the party to the socialization of industry, production and exchange. This was not an absurd idea. Australia at the time was well advanced on a path of import–replacement industrialization. This was exactly the strategy for peripheral economies urged by the famous UN think-tank CEPAL in Santiago de Chile and it was adopted in Australia by conservative politicians and capitalists as well as by Labor. Steel mills had been built, Holden cars were in production, the Snowy River was dammed for a great hydroelectric scheme, an industrial working class had come into existence. It was conceivable that this class would take control of economic growth.

That didn't happen. The local ruling class, backed by American and British capital, fought off the challenge. What working-class pressure did win, from the 1940s to the 1960s, was an Australian welfare state. This meant a social safety net and better housing for the white working class, Keynesian policies for full employment for men, and a tremendous expansion of public education for working-class children.

When the next wave of radical activism rose, it took unexpected directions. It was true that the New Left of the 1960s depended on the Old Left for organizational support, especially in contesting the horrifying war on Vietnam. Certain Labor Party leaders, notably Don Dunstan, Premier of South Australia, and Gough Whitlam, Prime Minister for three dramatic years in the 1970s, attracted some New Left energy into state-sponsored reforms.

But the main action was at the grass roots and this was fast and furious. A dozen years, from the mid 1960s to the late 1970s, saw the radicalization of students in the anti-war movement, the launching of Women's Liberation, an explosion of radical culture ranging from progressive rock to the Sydney Free University to the Melbourne experimental theatre the Pram Factory, new Aboriginal activism as the Land Rights movement got going, experiments in communal living such as the counter-cultural settlement at Nimbin in rural New South Wales, the Gay Liberation movement, attempts at workplace democracy, radical environmentalism and a green/red alliance as unions supported environmental actions. The revolution was suddenly more colourful.

There were no membership tickets in the New Left and no new Objective got printed. But there were overlaps between different campaigns, and common styles of action. The most important, to me, was a practice of direct democracy. This meant breaking down hierarchies, including socialist ones – no more vanguards. It meant trying to bring the new world into being, not by passing resolutions or pining for the October Revolution, but by actually doing it here and now – living your politics.

At its best, this made for wonderfully creative practice. Among the best (though not the best known) was the work of young progressive teachers. With some support from progressive bureaucrats (yes, they do exist!) teachers carved out space to involve children and communities in controlling their schools, to create more relevant curricula and develop livelier pedagogies. The Disadvantaged Schools Programme, launched in the mid 1970s, in schools surrounded by dire poverty with high proportions of migrant and indigenous children, produced some of the most inventive work in the entire history of Australian education.

When the New Left set out on its long march through the institutions, in Rudi Dutschke's memorable phrase, it did change the culture in major ways. It had a social base in the much-debated new middle class, as the Australian economy shifted towards service industries and levels of education rose.

But no mass organization came into existence around New Left agendas, not even Women's Liberation. The movement created no economic program. In the final analysis its dispersal across so many sites and projects made new-left radicalism vulnerable, when the dominant powers recovered from the defeat in Vietnam, the shock of youth revolt and the loss of control in institutions.

Reaction duly came. The neoliberal agenda, called 'economic rationalism' in Australia, meant privileging the managers, deregulating capital and labour markets, opening the local economy comprehensively to international capital, privatizing or starving the public sector and bloating private wealth. Just as industrial capitalism borrowed some socialist ideas for the Welfare State compromise in the 1950s, neoliberalism picked up some New Left ideas in the 1980s. It endorsed organizational flexibility, creativity and equal opportunity, but used these ideas to grow corporate wealth rather than to grow democracy.

Australian capitalism shifted gear again, from import–replacement industrialization to the search for comparative advantage in global markets – the signature strategy of neoliberalism on a world scale. The advantage was found, ironically for a newly industrialized country, by reverting to the colonial strategy of digging up and shipping out minerals while importing cheap manufactured goods. Red China, an object of paranoid fear in the 1950s, gradually became Australia's major trading partner. As Australia's industrial towns and suburbs began turning into rust belts, the labour movement groped for a strategy. There was another moment when the Left might have set the agenda and a union group tried to do just that in the 1987 report *Australia Reconstructed*.

But the moment was lost. More exactly it was seized by a machine politician from the most ruthless, corrupt and successful faction in the Labor Party: Paul Keating, treasurer in the Hawke Labor government. Keating's famous declaration of 1986, that if Australia did not become internationally competitive it would become a 'banana republic', crystallized the panic factor that drove Labor and the unions to the right. Keating and his allies crafted a strategy for the Labor Party to be the party of government within neoliberalism, riding the surf of market-driven change and even getting ahead of it.

In the global North, neoliberalism is linked with the names of Thatcher and Reagan; in Latin America, with the names of Pinochet and the International Monetary Fund. In New Zealand and Australia, it was labour parties that made the turn. The Australian Labor Party began selling off heavyweight public assets such as the national airline Qantas and the Commonwealth Bank. This happened with guidance from transnational management consultancies (who were making a mint from privatizations around the world) and the hidden complicity of public sector managers (who stood to gain a pot of money as private sector executives). The turn to the market went deep. By an alchemy never quite explained, prominent Labor leaders, both state and federal, began to reincarnate as millionaire businessmen and mates of developers, media moguls and financiers.

The current Labor agenda directly descends from the Keating strategy. There is little about it that is *not* neoliberal. It is completely in character that the banner strategy on climate change which brought the Rudd leadership undone in 2009–10 was an 'emissions trading scheme' – a device to allow corporations to buy and sell rights to pollute. This is a device that actually *prevents* popular control of the environment over the longer term.

The neoliberal turn has driven a split between parliamentary Labor and social movements (including the union movement) much deeper than in the 1970s. The party has no mass membership now that could serve as a connecting belt. Its membership numbers collapsed in the 1980s and 1990s. The Labor Party is more and more a shell company: a rentier of residual support from unionists and working-class communities and an entrepreneur in the world of corporate-funded media politics. It makes policy secretively at the top and its policy positions are announced when they are wanted by public relations strategy.

Social movements too have changed. Some entirely new political forms have emerged, such as blogging and Web-based organizing. The Obama campaign famously used on-line fundraising and campaign outreach; some social movements have also been very active on the Net. A deconstructive queer politics, that gained momentum in the 1990s, has invigorated debates around sexuality and identity. The environmental movement has more continuity, but it too evolves. In a key shift, environmental radicals began to target Australia's great contribution to global warming, coal exports. The attempt to create a new radical party, the Greens, has struggled to make an electoral breakthrough; it survives as a minority party, in 2010 won its first general-election seat in the House of Representatives, but has not found the kind of regional or class base on which the older parties grew. Yet the Greens have shown how to build democratic culture into a party machine.

Though there have been fresh starts like these, it has been increasingly difficult for the Left to mobilize on a broad basis, even when it seemed to have public support. Despite majority opinion against the Bush regime's invasion of Iraq, opponents of the war gained no political traction in 2003, when Australian troops were sent. At present there is hardly an audible voice against Australian soldiers killing people in Afghanistan – though some angst about Australian soldiers being killed. The Australian Left seems to be landlocked again. With all electorally credible parties neoliberal or worse and radical alternatives squeezed out of the public sphere, why would anyone want to be on the Left today?

Looking around: social reality now

When *Overland* began, it was easy to justify a commitment to the worker's republic. Workers were exploited and the capitalist system led to poverty and war. But the fantastic productivity of modern machine civilization could, under a different social system, make a good life for all. Some trusting souls even believed that the Soviets had already done it.

The world has turned and we have learned more about the bloody reality of Soviet government, as well as its cold-war opponents. We need to keep on learning, too. Any system of doctrine, any powerful concept, becomes in time an excuse for not thinking. Marxism, radical feminism, deconstructionism, postcolonialism, the lot.

This doesn't mean we should grab any new story that hits the airport bookstands. There is now a genre of pop sociology offering maps of a brave new world: the leisure society, the therapeutic society, the cyber-society, mega-trends, the creative classes and so on. Often they contain a little truth. But they are focused on the world's privileged and miss most of what is around us. We need harder thinking, not fluffier thinking, about social reality. That includes re-thinking the ideas earlier generations of socialists worked with.

Take, for instance, the concept 'the capitalist system', which still influences most socialist thought. Is global capitalism really a coherent *system*, grinding out growth or crisis by an inexorable logic, as both mainstream economics and Marxism suppose? I doubt it. World capitalism today looks more like an agglomeration of many qualitatively different structures of privilege, exploitation, brutality, theft and fraud, on which governments and transnational corporate managers are desperately trying to *impose* order.

Certainly, there are still horrible low-wage factories pumping out surplus-value, as Marx described in the famous chapter 15 of *Das Kapital*. But they are now in South China, Sri Lanka, northern Mexico or Vietnam, built on local patriarchies and authoritarian politics. Meanwhile Manchester, Pittsburgh and the Ruhr rust or become insurance hubs. It is not just a local economy of time, as Marx theorized, but five hundred years of imperialism that are vital to contemporary corporate strategies for generating profit. Neocolonialism, racial hierarchy and the exploitation of women all thrive and evolve. In front of your nose, as George Orwell remarked.

A lot of wealth-creation does not resemble the old surplus-value model at all. I'm not thinking only of pirates with their rusty Kalashnikovs off the coast of Somalia. I am also thinking of bankers and insurers in the fine glass towers of Sydney and Melbourne. Most observers agree that finance capital is central to the world economy nowadays. It displaced industrial capital in the lead role some decades ago and triggered the global crisis of 2008.

How do giant finance companies make their profits? Essentially, by running a system of private taxation. They skim a little tax of their own from each of the millions of transactions the economically active population can't avoid in everyday life – being paid, getting cash, using credit, having a house, running a car, insuring goods, funding superannuation and so on. Night and day, the skim floods in through the corporate computers. Remarkable. Much more efficient than Kalashnikovs. No wonder that the people who make these schemes work, the CEOs of the banks, brokers and insurers, are paid their tens of millions of dollars by grateful stakeholders.

We used to think that capital was one thing, the state was

another. But what do we make of China, or Singapore, or Saudi Arabia, or Dubai, now? In many parts of the world, to some extent in all parts of the world, the state has become a development machine. State action *generates* capital and profit, it does not just coordinate them. Negri was right about the 'enterprise-state' (chapter 9). The growth of sovereign wealth funds as major players in world finance is one sign of this. Another, in a small mean way, is the cabal of businessmen who for more than a decade ran the government of New South Wales in the name of Labor.

Around these development machines, a multinational ruling class of a new kind seems to be forming. This is a class privileged by education, wealth, language, political access and control of the means of violence. It is not united in strategy, as the fiasco of the Copenhagen climate conference in 2009 showed. But it is linked up by interwoven investments, and constant negotiations between the development machines. At a personal level, its members are linked by training (the MBA is emblematic), transnational careers, air travel, Louis Vuitton and secure electronic networks.

Peasants, migrant workers and favela dwellers – between them, half the world's population – have little access to the benefits. But the poor have full access to the environmental and industrial disasters these machines leave in their wake: mass poisoning in Bhopal, Chinese coal mines, giant dams, Mexico City air, the wrecking of the Niger delta, the chopping down of Sumatran forests . . . and global warming.

Australia is part of this world and in some respects a privileged part. Just before Christmas 2009 the *Sydney Morning Herald* published a column telling 'a few home truths' about Australia, written by its political editor Peter Hartcher, a right-wing journalist though not one of the paranoid ones. Hartcher recited the proof of Australia's good luck and good management, showing from official statistics and surveys that we are not only one of the richest countries in the world but also one of the fairest, with low income inequality, abounding opportunity and widespread happiness. Of course there are problems – Aboriginal Australia occurred to him – but we should count our blessings, because we live in 'a country of unsurpassed harmony and hope, that offers wide-open opportunity for the ambitious and a social safety net for those who fall by the wayside'.

This is pretty much the vision of Australian society on which all the major political parties agree, and it is a familiar story in North America and Europe too. In this story, the broad population are more or less equal and more or less content. Social problems only concern a minority who fall by the wayside. With the help of tough love and the Salvation Army they can be fixed through social inclusion. Politics is not about basic social change. It is about how to fuel, protect and steer the neoliberal development machine that now delivers prosperity.

No one who has looked at the figures will doubt that a large part of the Australian population is, by world standards, materially well off. Some are doing fabulously well: our corporate and professional elites are active players in the emerging world ruling class. Absolute poverty is limited; more Australians die in car crashes than die of starvation.

Let's add a few more reasons for pride. Australia kept at a very low level the HIV/AIDS epidemic, which became a social catastrophe in Africa and is an emerging crisis in south Asia. Australia built one of the best university systems in the world – a little surprising that, for a famously anti-intellectual country. Over several generations, Australia built one of the strongest systems of protection for workers' rights. In the last generation a functioning system of indigenous land rights has been created, a dramatic break from earlier Australian history.

These blessings were hard to get and are not guaranteed to last. A high level of HIV prevention was achieved by painstaking mobilization and education in a grief-stricken gay community. The university system, which we owe to popular pressure and the hard work of two generations of Australian academics, is currently being torn apart by neoliberalism. Part of the workers' protection system has gone and a weakened union movement isn't able to win much back. Aboriginal land rights were overridden, in the Northern Territory, by a startlingly authoritarian policy shift in 2007 called 'the intervention' into Aboriginal communities, which got bipartisan support in the national parliament.

What Australia has of wider prosperity, then, isn't a gift from our ruling class, smiling benevolently from their yachts. It was won by social struggles, of many different kinds, and it is based on the daily labour put in by millions of workers who don't wear Prada and don't make stock market killings. In the final analysis, we should not get complacent about Australian affluence because we don't live alone. 'Australia' as an economy now effectively includes the Korean workers who stoke the furnaces burning Australian coal, the Indian workers who answer call centres for Australian firms, and the Malaysian workers who generate the profits to pay Australian university fees for their employers' children. No country is an island, entire of itself.

It is the unequal distribution of power, resources and respect on a global scale with which, ultimately, the Left has to grapple. And it is on that scale that we now confront a neoliberal order where development machines and corporate power have, in the late twentieth and early twenty-first century, broken free of most social and cultural restraints. This is having long-term environmental effects that few of us can bear to think about. In the much shorter term it produces strategies that amount to support for mass murder.

How else can we regard the modern arms industry, worth more than fifty billion dollars a year in international trade alone, that equips armies, militias, dictatorships, mafias and domestic violence around the world? How else can we regard the pharmaceutical industry that priced antiretroviral medication out of reach of the world's poor while the AIDS epidemic grew to devastating size? What can we say about the states and corporations that built a playground for the global rich in Dubai behind a rampart of half a million dead in Iraq? And what could anyone say about the states and corporations that built the 23 000 nuclear warheads that currently exist?

Looking forward

The world does not have to be this way. That is the basic case for the Left and always has been. The violence and insecurity, the exploitation and inequality, the corruption of culture, the threats to the future of the planet, are the work of humans, not the law of God. And what humans have built, we can build otherwise. *Otro mundo es posible.*

How? I once thought we could lay down a Plan. In fact, I once wrote a bright red pamphlet, *Socialism and Labor: An Australian Strategy*, which solemnly tried to wrap Old Left and New Left together in one package and show it could be a juke-box hit. That one went into the dustbin of history.

We still need to be concerned with practicalities, with how social and economic structures might actually change and be made to work. The next Left therefore has to be concerned with economic life, with how the needs of working-class and peasant families can be met, and how the mechanisms for meeting needs can operate democratically.

The bases for economic democracy are already here. Despite the rhetoric of competition and individual entrepreneurship, most goods and services are actually produced through cooperation. It is workers' know-how and inventiveness that make a capitalist economy function, day by day.

We have many models of cooperative labour. There is a rich international and local history, ranging from cooperative child-care centres, to farm and craft production, to Internet share-ware. Among current experiments are the factories in Argentina that were occupied and run by their workers when threatened with closure under neoliberal restructuring. Some later got government support that gave them legal stability.

How can cooperative forms of labour scale up to the size of a whole economy, especially in an environment of neoliberal globalization? No one has done that yet. The most exciting work on this issue now seems to be happening in Latin America. In Bolivia, Ecuador and Venezuela, for instance, progressive governments operate in an environment of mobilized social movements. A new era in indigenous politics has emerged here. In this region, neoliberalism is being more frontally challenged than anywhere else in the world.

The Australian Left, like the rest of the country, habitually takes its political and cultural cues from Europe and North America. In the 1950s this attitude was called the 'cultural cringe' and *Overland* made a protest against it. The instinct was sound, but we need a wider base. In many ways Australia's economic and cultural situation parallels that of other countries in the global periphery. Building connections here matters. Some of the most penetrating social and political thought of the past two decades has come from India, South Africa, Mexico and Brazil.

A democratized economy means not only changes within individual workplaces, but a drive for equality and security on the larger scale. A basic feature of neoliberal society is manufactured insecurity. This is the dark underside of competition and the cult of the entrepreneur. Until there is secure employment and secure entitlement to services – centrally, health, education and housing – we do not have much chance of shifting the long hours culture, unequal gender division of labour, or racism. Australia does not suffer from any lack of resources to make secure and healthy lives. We do need a different design of institutions.

The Women's Liberation movement opened up issues about the politics of intimacy, including the politics of bodies, that have been explored creatively ever since. One of the liveliest movements in the last couple of decades has been queer politics, with young people doing surprising and inventive things to disrupt oppressive norms. I'm sure that a radical politics of embodiment will continue and I think it will be particularly important if it connects with the politics of care.

This doesn't mean New Age sentimentality. 'Care' means a quality of practice in social relations: loving child-care, good neighbourhoods and good sexual relationships. It is a quality common to feminist work against domestic violence and femicide, struggles for forest protection, and attempts at healing in the aftermath of colonialism and war. There isn't a peace movement in the old sense any more. But some of its threads continue.

One of the important lessons about care, particularly taught by the women's movement, is that a movement for change needs to care for its activists. To challenge power is always a bruising experience and sometimes worse than that. All the major development machines are violent, buttressed by police and military force. A movement for change has to be sustainable over the long haul and some forms of radical activism are not. In fact, in past generations the Left tended to chew up and spit out its activists. We need to give honour to the support work and the support workers, and find ways of doing change that generate care relations within a movement.

Cultural politics has been a great field of invention and upheaval in the last generation. We are still coming to terms with the idea of plural cultures and multiple knowledge systems. New technologies, hyped and commercialized as they are, have great possibilities for decentralized sharing of ideas. Yet we haven't exhausted the democratic potential of old technologies, the bicycles of the cultural world. This is why I value projects like *Overland* magazine, still exploring the edges between new writing and radical politics, as it steps into a digital era while keeping the power of print alive.

A sustainable movement for democratic change needs imagination. We do not want blueprints any more; we expect to feel our way into the future. But we certainly need utopian thinking, the capacity to break out of the given, to find beauty, to create symbols. The Waratahs matter, as well as the Bread.

Acknowledgements

Most of the chapters in this book are based on articles contributed to journals and books, some of which are not widely available. All have been re-written for this book. I thank the editors, reviewers and publishers of: 'Periphery and metropole in the history of sociology', *Sociologisk Forskning*, 2010, vol. 47 no. 1, 72–86; 'Bread and waratahs', *Overland*, 2010, no. 198, 17–24; 'Good teachers on dangerous ground: towards a new view of teacher quality and professionalism', *Critical Studies in Education*, 2009, vol. 50 no. 3, 213–29 http://informaworld.com; 'The neoliberal parent: mothers and fathers in the new market society', pp. 26–40 in Paula-Irene Villa and Barbara Thiessen, eds, *Mütter – Väter: Diskurse, Medien, Praxen*, Münster, Westfälisches Dampfboot, 2009; 'The experience of gender change in public sector organizations', *Gender Work and Organization*, 2006, vol. 13 no. 5, 435–52 © Raewyn Connell, © 2006 Blackwell Publishing Ltd; 'Empire, domination, autonomy: Antonio Negri as a social theorist', *Overland*, 2005, no. 181, 31–9; 'Change among the gatekeepers: men, masculinities, and gender equality in the global arena', *Signs*, 2005, vol. 30 no. 3, 1801–25 © 2005 by the University of Chicago; 'Not the Pyramids: intellectual work and its politics in a neoliberal era', *Dialogue*

(Academy of the Social Sciences in Australia), 2005, vol. 24 no. 1, 17–26; 'Working-class families and the new secondary education', *Australian Journal of Education*, 2003, vol. 47 no. 3, 237–52 (published by the Australian Council for Educational Research).

I am grateful to June Crawford and Julian Wood, colleagues in the studies discussed in chapter 6; to Toni Schofield and Sue Goodwin, colleagues in the study discussed in chapter 2; to Stephen Crump and Gordon Stanley, colleagues in the study discussed in chapter 4. I am pleased to acknowledge grants from the Australian Research Council re chapters 2, 4 and 6, from the NSW Premier's Department and other agencies (which cannot be named for confidentiality reasons) re chapter 2, and the NSW Department of Education and Training and the Board of Studies re chapter 4. Chapter 5 builds on ideas from many contributors to the 2008 'Good Teacher' seminars at the University of Sydney, particularly Craig Campbell, Susan Groundwater-Smith, Jo-Anne Reid, Lesley Scanlon, Terri Seddon and Tony Welch. Re chapter 2, I am grateful to project staff Kathy Edwards, Celia Roberts, Virginia Watson and Julian Wood, industry partners Philippa Hall and Jennifer Perry, and agency representatives. Re chapter 4, I am grateful to project staff David Saltmarsh, Gill Yates, Deborah Youdell, Megan Lugg and Camilla Couch, and to many staff of the public education system. Opinions expressed in these chapters are those of the author alone and do not necessarily reflect the view of any participating agency. Some interviews in chapter 6 were conducted by Renate Kretschmer, and the field survey was conducted by Market Equity Pty Ltd; thanks to Ian Stewart and Roy Jopson. I also owe much to people who have created occasions for thought and writing, especially Paula Villa and Barbara Thiessen, Per Wisselgren, and Nathan Hollier. John Fisher has been my research assistant through most of this work and his bibliographical work underlies chapters 1, 3 and 7. Jonathan Skerrett of Polity Press is the commissioning editor and I am grateful for his enthusiasm for this project and help in shaping it; Elizabeth Weiss of Allen and Unwin Australia has supported my work with judgement and care over many years.

Beyond this, all I can say is that intellectual work is a highly social product, so I am grateful to far more colleagues than I can possibly name. Intellectual work is also personally demanding, so I am grateful to friends and family who have given vital support, above all, Kylie Benton-Connell and Patricia Selkirk.

References

Acker, Joan. 1990. 'Hierarchies, bodies and jobs: a gendered theory of organisations'. *Gender and Society* 4(2): 139–58.

Acker, Sandra. 1983. 'Women and teaching: a semi-detached sociology of a semi-profession', pp. 123–39 in Stephen Walker and Len Barton, eds, *Gender, Class and Education*. Lewes, Sussex: Falmer Barcombe.

Adesina, Jimi O. 2002. 'Sociology and Yoruba studies: epistemic intervention or doing sociology in the "vernacular"?' *African Sociological Review/Revue Africaine de Sociologie* 6(1): 91–114.

Akiwowo, Akinsola A. 1980. 'Sociology in Africa today', *Current Sociology* 28(2): 1–73.

   1986. 'Contributions to the sociology of knowledge from an African oral poetry', *International Sociology* 1(4): 343–58.

   1999. 'Indigenous sociologies: extending the scope of the argument', *International Sociology* 14(2): 115–38.

Al-Afghani, Sayyid Jamal ad-Din. [1881] 1968. *An Islamic Response to Imperialism: Political and Religious Writings of Sayyid Jamal ad-Din 'al-Afghani'*. Translated by Nikki R. Keddie and Hamid Algar. Berkeley: University of California Press.

Alatas, Syed Hussein. 2006. 'The autonomous, the universal and the future of sociology', *Current Sociology* 54(1): 7–23.

Al-e Ahmad, Jalal. [1962]1982. *Gharbzadegi (Weststruckness)*. Translated by John Green and Ahmad Alizadeh. Lexington, KY: Mazda Publishers.

Altman, Dennis. 1994. *Power and Community: Organizational and Cultural Responses to AIDS*. London: Taylor and Francis.

Amin, Samir. 1974. *Accumulation on a World Scale: A Critique of the Theory of Underdevelopment*. New York: Monthly Review Press.

　　　1997. *Capitalism in the Age of Globalization: The Management of Contemporary Society*. London: Zed Books.

Anderson, Francis. 1912. *Sociology in Australia: A Plea for its Teaching*. Sydney: Angus and Robertson.

Anderson, Kay. 2007. *Race and the Crisis of Humanism*. London: Routledge.

Apple, Michael W. 1993. *Official Knowledge*. New York: Routledge.

Asad, Talal, ed. 1973. *Anthropology and the Colonial Encounter*. New York: Humanities Press.

Bacchi, Carol and Joan Eveline. 2010. 'Introduction: mainstreaming politics, gendering practices and feminist theory', in Carol Bacchi and Joan Eveline, eds, *Mainstreaming and Neoliberalism: a Contested Relationship*. Adelaide: The University of Adelaide Press.

Baehr, Peter. 2002. *Founders, Classics, Canons: Modern Disputes over the Origins and Appraisal of Sociology's Heritage*. New Brunswick: Transaction Publishers.

Bakare-Yusuf, Bibi. 2003. '"Yorubas don't do gender": a critical review of Oyeronke Oyewumi's *The Invention of Women: Making an African Sense of Western Gender Discourses*', *African Identities* 1(1): 121–42.

Balandier, Georges. [1955] 1970. *The Sociology of Black Africa: Social Dynamics in Central Africa*. London: André Deutsch.

Balme, Jane and Sandra Bowdler. 2006. 'Spear and digging stick: the origin of gender and its implications for the colonization of new continents', *Journal of Social Archaeology* 6(3): 379–401.

Barley, Stephen R. and Gideon Kunda. 2004. *Gurus, Hired Guns and Warm Bodies: Itinerant Experts in a Knowledge Economy*. Princeton: Princeton University Press.

Bauman, Zygmunt. 1987. *Legislators and Interpreters*. Ithaca, NY: Cornell University Press.

Beck, Ulrich. 1999. *World Risk Society*. Cambridge: Polity.

Becker, Gary S. 1981. *A Treatise on the Family*. Cambridge, MA: Harvard University Press.

Benda, Julien. 1928. *The Great Betrayal [La trahison des clercs]*. London: Routledge.

Berman, Edward H. 1983. *The Influence of the Carnegie, Ford and Rockefeller Foundations on American Foreign Policy: the Ideology of Philanthropy*. Albany: State University of New York Press.

Bettie, Julie. 2002. *Women Without Class*. Berkeley: University of California Press.

Bezanson, Kate and Meg Luxton, eds. 2006. *Social Reproduction: Feminist Political Economy Challenges Neo-liberalism*. Montreal and Kingston: McGill-Queen's University Press.

Bezuidenhout, Andries and Khayaat Fakier. 2006. 'Maria's burden: Contract cleaning and the crisis of social reproduction in post-Apartheid South Africa', *Antipode* 38(3): 462–85.

Bittman, Michael and Jocelyn Pixley. 1997. *The Double Life of the Family: Myth, Hope and Experience*. Sydney: Allen and Unwin.

Bjerrum Nielsen, Harriet and Monica Rudberg. 1994. *Psychological Gender and Modernity*. Oslo: Scandinavian University Press.

Bly, Robert. 1990. *Iron John: A Book about Men*. Reading: Addison-Wesley.

Borchorst, Anette. 1999. 'Feminist thinking about the welfare state', pp. 99 – 127 in Myra Marx Ferree, Judith Lorber and Beth B. Hess, eds, *Revisioning Gender*. Thousand Oaks, CA: Sage Publications.

Bourdieu, Pierre and Jean-Claude Passeron. 1977. *Reproduction in education, society and culture*. London and Beverly Hills: Sage Publications.

Brannen, Julia and Ann Nilsen. 2006. 'From fatherhood to fathering: transmission and change among British fathers in four-generation families', *Sociology* 40(2): 335–52.

Breines, Ingeborg, Raewyn Connell and Ingrid Eide, eds. 2000. *Male Roles, Masculinities and Violence: A Culture of Peace Perspective*. Paris: UNESCO Publishing.

Brennan, Deborah. 2002. 'Australia: child care and state-centered feminism in a liberal welfare regime', pp. 95–112 in Sonya Michel and Rianne Mahon, eds, *Child Care Policy at the Crossroads: Gender and Welfare State Restructuring*. New York: Routledge.

Bukharin, Nikolai. [1925]1965. *Historical Materialism: A System of Sociology.* New York: Russell and Russell.

Bulbeck, Chilla. 1998. *Re-Orienting Western Feminisms: Women's Diversity in a Postcolonial World.* Cambridge: Cambridge University Press.

Burawoy, Michael. 2005. 'For public sociology', *American Sociological Review* 70(1): 4–28.

Burawoy, Michael, Mau-kuei Chang and Michelle Fei-yu Hsieh, eds. 2010. *Facing an Unequal World: Challenges for a Global Sociology.* Taipei: Academia Sinica.

Burton, Clare. 1987. 'Merit and gender: organisations and the mobilisation of masculine bias', *Australian Journal of Social Issues* 22(2): 424–35.

Business Council of Australia. 2008. *Teaching Talent: The Best Teachers for Australia's Classrooms.* Melbourne: Business Council of Australia.

Camic, Charles and Neil Gross. 2001. 'The new sociology of ideas', pp. 236–49 in Judith R. Blau, ed., *The Blackwell Companion to Sociology.* Oxford: Blackwell.

Cardoso, Fernando Henrique and Enzo Faletto. [1971] 1979. *Dependency and Development in Latin America.* Berkeley: University of California Press.

Childe, Vere Gordon. 1960. *What Happened in History*, rev. edn. London: Parrish.

Chopra, Radhika, ed. 2002. *From Violence to Supportive Practice: Family, Gender and Masculinities in India.* New Delhi: UNIFEM (United Nations Development Fund for Women).

Clark, Judith. 2003. *To Hell in a Handcart: Educational Realities, Teachers' Work and Neoliberal Restructuring in NSW TAFE.* PhD thesis, University of Sydney, Faculty of Education.

Clark, Marshall. 2010. *Maskulinitas: Culture, Gender and Politics in Indonesia.* Melbourne: MAI Press.

Clawson, Dan *et al.* 2007. *Public Sociology: Fifteen Eminent Sociologists Debate Politics and the Profession in the Twenty-first Century.* Berkeley: University of California Press.

Coakley, Jay. 2006. 'The good father: parental expectations and youth sports', *Leisure Studies* 259(2): 153–63.

Cockburn, Cynthia. 2010. 'Gender relations as causal in militarization and war', *International Feminist Journal of Politics* 12(2): 139–57.

Collier, Richard. 2010. *Men, Law and Gender: Essays on the 'Man' of Law.* Abingdon: Routledge.

Collins, Randall. 1997. 'A sociological guilt trip: comment on Connell', *American Journal of Sociology* 102(6): 1558–64.

Collinson, David L. and Jeff Hearn, eds. 1996. *Men as Managers, Managers as Men: Critical Perspectives on Men, Masculinities and Managements.* London: Sage.

Compton, Mary and Lois Weiner. 2008. *The Global Assault on Teaching, Teachers and their Unions: Stories for Resistance.* New York: Palgrave Macmillan.

Connell, Raewyn. 1977. *Ruling Class, Ruling Culture.* Cambridge: Cambridge University Press.

1985. *Teachers' Work.* Sydney: Allen and Unwin.

1995. 'Transformative labour: theorizing the politics of teachers' work', pp. 91–114 in Mark B. Ginsburg, ed., *The politics of educators' work and lives.* New York: Garland Publishing.

1997. 'Why is classical theory classical?', *American Journal of Sociology* 102(6): 1511–57.

2003a. 'Scrambling in the ruins of patriarchy: neo-liberalism and men's divided interests in gender change', pp. 58–69 in Ursula Pasero, ed., *Gender: from Costs to Benefits.* Wiesbaden: Westdeutscher Verlag.

2003b. 'Men, gender and the state', pp. 15–28 in Søren Ervø and Thomas Johansson, eds, *Among Men: Moulding Masculinities*, vol. 1. Aldershot: Ashgate.

2005a. *Masculinities.* 2nd edn. Berkeley and Los Angeles, CA: University of California Press

2005b. 'A really good husband: work/life balance, gender equity and social change', *Australian Journal of Social Issues* 40(3): 369–83.

2007. *Southern Theory: The Global Dynamics of Knowledge in Social Science.* Sydney: Allen and Unwin; Cambridge: Polity.

2009. *Gender: In World Perspective.* 2nd edn. Cambridge: Polity.

2010. 'Im Innern des gläsernen Turms: Die Konstruktion von Männlichkeiten im Finanzkapital', *Feministische Studien* 28(1): 8–24.

Connell, Raewyn, Dean Ashenden, Sandra Kessler and Gary Dowsett. 1982. *Making the Difference: Schools, Families and Social Division.* Sydney: Allen and Unwin.

Connell, Raewyn and Julian Wood. 2005. 'Globalization and business masculinities', *Men and Masculinities* 7(4): 347–64.

Connell, W. F. and nine others. 1962. *The Foundations of Education*. Sydney: Ian Novak.

Crowley, Helen and Susan Himmelweit, eds. 1992. *Knowing Women: Feminism and Knowledge*. Cambridge: Polity and Open University.

Cupples, Julie. 2005. 'Love and money in an age of neoliberalism: gender, work and single motherhood in postrevolutionary Nicaragua', *Environment and Planning A* 37: 305–22.

Davies, Bronwyn. 1993. *Shards of Glass: Children Reading and Writing beyond Gender Identities*. Sydney: Allen and Unwin Australia.

Deleuze, Gilles and Felix Guattari. [1980] 1988. *A Thousand Plateaus: Capitalism and Schizophrenia*. London: Athlone Press.

Deutscher, Max. 1983. *Subjecting and Objecting: An Essay in Objectivity*. Oxford: Basil Blackwell Publisher Limited.

Division for the Advancement of Women, Department of Economic and Social Affairs, United Nations. 2008. *The Role of Men and Boys in Achieving Gender Equality*. December 2008 issue of *Women 2000 and Beyond*, available online at http://www.un.org/womenwatch/daw/public/w2000.html.

Doherty, Robert A. and Margery A. McMahon. 2007. 'Politics, change and compromise: restructuring the work of the Scottish teacher', *Educational Review*, 59(3): 251–65.

Donaldson, Mike. 1991. *Time of Our Lives: Labour and Love in the Working Class*. Sydney: Allen and Unwin.

Donaldson, Mike and Scott Poynting. 2007. *Ruling Class Men: Money, Sex, Power*. Bern: Peter Lang.

Donner, Henrike. 2006. 'Committed mothers and well-adjusted children: privatisation, early years education and motherhood in Calcutta', *Modern Asian Studies*, 40(2): 371–95.

Duménil, Gérard and Dominique Lévy. 2004. *Capital Resurgent: Roots of the Neoliberal Revolution*. Cambridge, MA: Harvard University Press.

Eisenstein, Hester. 1996. *Australian Femocrats and the State*. Sydney: Allen and Unwin.

2009. *Feminism Seduced: How Global Elites Use Women's Labor and Ideas to Exploit the World*. Boulder, CO: Paradigm Publishers.

Estola, Eila and Freema Elbaz-Luwisch. 2003. 'Teaching bodies at work', *Journal of Curriculum Studies* 35(6): 697–719.

Ferguson, Harry. 2001. 'Men and masculinities in late-modern Ireland', pp. 118–134 in Bob Pease and Keith Pringle, eds, *A Man's World? Changing Men's Practices in a Globalized World*. London: Zed Books.

Frank, Blye W. and Kevin G. Davison. 2007. *Masculinities and Schooling: International Practices and Perspectives*. London and Ontario: Althouse Press.

Franzway, Suzanne. 2001. *Sexual Politics and Greedy Institutions*. Sydney: Pluto Press.

Fuller, Norma. 2001. 'The social constitution of gender identity among Peruvian men', *Men and Masculinities* 3(3): 316–31.

Garretón, Manuel Antonio. 2000. *La sociedad in que vivi(re)mos: Introduccion sociológica al cambio de siglo*. Santiago: LOM.

Ghamari-Tabrizi, Behrooz. 1996. 'Is Islamic science possible?' *Social Epistemology*, 10(3–4): 317–30.

Giddens, Anthony. 2002. *Runaway World: How Globalisation is Reshaping our Lives*, new edn. London: Profile Books.

Gilding, Michael. 1997. *Australian Families: A Comparative Perspective*. Melbourne: Longman.

Gill, Lesley. 2000. *Teetering on the Rim: Global Restructuring, Daily Life and the Armed Retreat of the Bolivian State*. New York: Columbia University Press.

Ginsborg, Paul. 1990. *A History of Contemporary Italy: Society and Politics 1943–1988*. London: Penguin.

Giroux, H. A. 1988. *Teachers as Intellectuals: Toward a Critical Pedagogy of Learning*. Granby, MA: Bergin and Garvey.

Gouldner, Alvin. 1979. *The Future of Intellectuals and the Rise of the New Class*. New York: Continuum.

Grace, Gerald. 1978. *Teachers, Ideology and Control: A Study in Urban Education*. London: Routledge and Kegan Paul.

Gutmann, Matthew C. 2002. *The Romance of Democracy: Compliant Defiance in Contemporary Mexico*. Berkeley: University of California Press.

Gyekye, Kwame. 1987. *An Essay on African Philosophical Thought: The Akan Conceptual Scheme*. Cambridge: Cambridge University Press.

Han, Clara. 2004. 'The work of indebtedness: the traumatic present of late capitalist Chile', *Culture, Medicine and Psychiatry* 28(2): 169–87.

Hardt, Michael and Antonio Negri. 1994. *Labor of Dionysus: A Critique of the State-Form*. Minneapolis: University of Minnesota Press.

2000. *Empire*. Cambridge, MA: Harvard University Press.

[2004] 2005. *Multitude: War and Democracy in the Age of Empire*. London: Hamish Hamilton.

Harrison, James. 1978. 'Warning: The male sex role may be dangerous to your health', *Journal of Social Issues* 34(1): 65–86.

Harvey, David. 2005. *A Brief History of Neoliberalism*. Oxford: Oxford University Press.

Hau'ofa, Epeli. 2008. *We Are the Ocean*. Honolulu: University of Hawaii Press.

Hearn, Jeff. 1998. *The Violences of Men: How Men Talk About and How Agencies Respond to Men's Violence to Women*. Thousand Oaks, CA: Sage Publications.

Hebson, Gail, Jill Earnshaw and Lorrie Marchington. 2007. 'Too emotional to be capable? The changing nature of emotion work in definitions of "capable teaching"', *Journal of Education Policy* 22(6): 675–94.

Hill, Elizabeth. 2006. 'Howard's "choice": the ideology and politics of work and family policy 1996–2006', *Australian Review of Public Affairs*, 23 (Feb 2006), http://www.australianreview.net/digest/2006/02/hill.html, accessed 19 June 2007.

Hoadley, Ursula. 2003. 'Time to learn: pacing and the external framing of teachers' work'. *Journal of Education for Teaching*, 29(3): 265–74.

Holland, Janet, Caroline Ramazanoglu, Sue Sharpe and Rachel Thomson. 1998. *The Male in the Head: Young People, Heterosexuality and Power*. London: Tufnell Press.

Holter, Øystein Gullvåg. 1995. 'Family theory reconsidered', 99–129 in Tordis Borchgrevink and Øystein Gullvåg Holter, eds, *Labour of Love: Beyond the Self-Evidence of Everyday Life*. Aldershot: Avebury.

1997. *Gender, Patriarchy and Capitalism: A Social Forms Analysis*. Oslo: Work Research Institute.

2003. *Can Men Do It? Men and Gender Equality – The Nordic Experience*. Copenhagen: Nordic Council of Ministers.

Hopenhayn, Martin. 2001. *No apocalypse, no integration: Modernism and postmodernism in Latin America*. Durham: Duke University Press.

Hountondji, Paulin J. 1973. *Libertés: Contribution à la Révolution Dahoméenne*. Cotonou: Editions Renaissance.

[1976] 1983. *African Philosophy: Myth and Reality*. Trans. H. Evans and J. Rée. London: Hutchinson.

1990. 'Pour une sociologie des représentations collectives', pp. 187–192 in Berthoud, Gérald *et al.*, eds, *La Pensée metisse*. Paris: PUF.

1995. 'Producing knowledge in Africa today', *African Studies Review* 38(3): 1–10.

1996. 'Intellectual responsibility: implications for thought and action today', *Proceedings and Addresses of the American Philosophical Association* 70(2): 77–92.

[1994] 1997. 'Introduction: recentring Africa', pp. 1–39 in Paulin J. Hountondji, ed., *Endogenous Knowledge: Research Trails*. Dakar: CODESRIA.

2002. *The Struggle for Meaning: Reflections on Philosophy, Culture and Democracy in Africa*. Athens, OH: Ohio University Press.

Hountondji, Paulin J. ed. 2007. *La rationalité, une ou plurielle?* Dakar: CODESRIA.

Hountondji, Paulin J., V. Y. Mudimbe and K. A. Appiah. 1991. 'Educating Africa', *Transition* 54: 156–64.

Hurrelmann, Klaus and Petra Kolip, eds. 2002. *Geschlecht, Gesundheit und Krankheit: Männer und Frauen im Vergleich*. Bern: Verlag Hans Huber.

Hyams, B. K. 1979. *Teacher preparation in Australia: A history of its development from 1850 to 1950*. Melbourne: ACER.

Imam, Ayesha, Amina Mama and Fatou Sow, eds. 1997. *Engendering African Social Sciences*. Dakar: CODESRIA.

Johnson, Vivien. 2008. *Lives of the Papunya Tula Artists*. Alice Springs: IAD Press.

Jolly, Margaret. 2008. 'The south in Southern Theory: Antipodean reflections on the Pacific', *Australian Humanities Review* 44 (online).

Kagamé, Alexis. 1976. *La philosophie bantu comparée*. Paris: Présence Africaine.

Kandiyoti, Deniz. 1994. 'The paradoxes of masculinity: some thoughts on segregated societies', pp. 197–213 in Andrea Cornwall and Nancy

Lindisfarne, eds, *Dislocating Masculinity: Comparative Ethnographies*. London: Routledge.

Kartini, Raden Adjeng. 2005. *On Feminism and Nationalism: Kartini's Letters to Stella Zeehandelaar, 1899–1903*. Clayton: Monash University Press.

Kay, Cristóbal. 1989. *Latin American Theories of Development and Underdevelopment*. London: Routledge.

Kenyatta, Jomo. 1938. *Facing Mount Kenya: The Tribal Life of the Gikuyu*. London: Secker and Warburg.

Kiernan, Victor G. 1969. *The Lords of Human Kind: Black Man, Yellow Man and White Man in an Age of Empire*. Boston: Little and Brown.

Kimmel, Michael S., Jeff Hearn and Raewyn Connell, eds. 2005. *Handbook of Studies on Men and Masculinities*. Thousand Oaks, CA: Sage Publication.

Kindler, Heinz. 2002. *Väter und Kinder*. Juventa: Weinheim and München.

Kippax, Susan, Raewyn Connell, Gary Dowsett and June Crawford. 1993. *Sustaining Safe Sex: Gay Communities Respond to AIDS*. London: Falmer Press.

Kleinhenz, Elizabeth and Lawrence Ingvarson. 2004. 'Teacher accountability in Australia: current policies and practices and their relation to the improvement of teaching and learning', *Research Papers in Education* 19(1): 31–49.

Konrád, George, and Ivan Szelényi. 1979. *The Intellectuals on the Road to Class Power: A Sociological Study of the Role of the Intelligentsia in Socialism*. New York: Harcourt Brace Jovanovich.

Kosík, Karel. 1976. *Dialectics of the Concrete*. Dordrecht: D. Reidel.

Kozlarek, Oliver. 2009. 'The sociology of Octavio Paz', pp. 137–54 in Oliver Kozlarek, ed., *Octavio Paz: Humanism and Critique*. Bielefeld: Transcript Verlag.

Kuznesof, Elizabeth. 2005. 'The house, the street, global society: Latin American families and childhood in the twenty-first century', *Journal of Social History* 38(4): 859–72.

Latour, Bruno and Steve Woolgar (1979) *Laboratory Life: The Social Construction of Scientific Facts*. Beverly Hills, CA: Sage .

Lingard, Bob. 2003. 'Where to in gender policy in education after recuperative masculinity politics?', *International Journal of Inclusive Education* 7(1): 33–56.

Lukács, Gyorgy. [1923] 1971. *History and Class Consciousness: Studies in Marxist Dialectics*. London: Merlin Press.

Lyotard, Jean-François. 1984. *The Postmodern Condition: A Report on Knowledge*. Minneapolis: University of Minnesota Press.

Mac an Ghaill, Mairtin. 1994. *The Making of Men: Masculinities, Sexualities and Schooling*. Buckingham: Open University Press.

Mackie, Alexander, ed. 1924. *The Groundwork of Teaching*. Sydney: Teachers' College Press and Angus and Robertson.

McMahon, Anthony. 1999. *Taking Care of Men: Sexual Politics in the Public Mind*. Cambridge: Cambridge University Press.

Mannheim, Karl. [1929] 1985. *Ideology and Utopia: An Introduction to the Sociology of Knowledge*. San Diego: Harcourt Brace Jovanovich.

[1935] 1940. *Man and Society in an Age of Reconstruction*. London: Kegan Paul.

1951. *Freedom, Power and Democratic Planning*. London: Routledge and Kegan Paul.

Mannon, Susan E. 2006. 'Love in the time of neo-liberalism: gender, work and power in a Costa Rican marriage', *Gender and Society* 20(4): 511–30.

Martin, William G. and Mark Beittel. 1998. 'Toward a global sociology? Evaluating current conceptions, methods and practices', *Sociological Quarterly* 39(1): 139–61.

Maunier, René. [1932] 1949. *The Sociology of Colonies: An Introduction to the Study of Race Contact*. London: Routledge and Kegan Paul.

Mealyea, R. 1993. Reproducing vocationalism in secondary schools: marginalization in practical workshops. In L. Angas, ed., *Education, Inequality and Social Identity*. London: Falmer.

Menzu Senta [Men's Center Japan]. 1997. *Otokotachi no watashisagashi [How are men seeking their new selves?]*. Kyoto: Kamogawa.

Messner, Michael A. 1997. *The Politics of Masculinities: Men in Movements*. Thousand Oaks, CA: Sage Publications.

2002. *Taking the Field: Women, Men and Sports*. Minneapolis: University of Minnesota Press.

2007. *Out of Play: Critical Essays on Gender and Sport*. Albany: State University of New York Press.

Metz-Göckel, Sigrid and Ursula Müller. 1985. *Der Mann: Die Brigitte-Studie*. Hamburg: Beltz.

Meuser, Michael. 2003. 'Modernized masculinities? Continuities, challenges and changes in men's lives', pp. 127–48 in Søren Ervø and Thomas Johansson, eds, *Among Men: Moulding Masculinities*, vol. 1. Aldershot: Ashgate.

Mills, Martin. 2004. 'The media, marketing and single sex schooling', *Journal of Education Policy* 19 no. 3, 343–60.

Mkandawire, Thandika. 2005. 'African intellectuals and nationalism', pp. 10–55 in Mkandawire T., ed., *African Intellectuals: Rethinking Politics, Language, Gender and Development*. Dakar: CODESRIA Books and London: Zed Books.

Moghadam, Valentine M. 2005. *Globalizing Women: Transnational Feminist Networks*. Baltimore: Johns Hopkins University Press.

Mohanty, Chandra Talpade. 2003. *Feminism Without Borders: Decolonizing Theory, Practicing Solidarity*. Durham: Duke University Press.

Mohwald, Ulrich. 2002. *Changing Attitudes towards Gender Equality in Japan and Germany*. München: Iudicium.

Moodie, T. Dunbar. 1994. *Going for Gold: Men, Mines and Migration*. Johannesburg: Witwatersrand University Press.

Moore, Alex. 2004. *The Good Teacher: Dominant Discourses in Teaching and Teacher Education*. Abingdon: Routledge.

Morrell, Robert, ed. 2001a. *Changing Men in Southern Africa*. Pietermaritzburg, South Africa: University of Natal Press.

2001b. *From Boys to Gentlemen: Settler Masculinity in Colonial Natal, 1880–1920*. Pretoria: University of South Africa Press.

Nandy, Ashis. 1983. *The Intimate Enemy: Loss and Recovery of Self under Colonialism*. New Delhi: Oxford University Press.

Nascimento, Elisa Larkin. 2007. *The Sorcery of Color: Identity, Race and Gender in Brazil*. Philadelphia, Temple University Press.

Negri, Antonio. 1974a. *Crisi dello stato-piano: comunismo e organizzazione rivoluzionaria*. Milano: Feltrinelli.

1974b. 'Partito operaio contro il lavoro', pp. 99–193 in Sergio Bologna, Paolo Carpignano and Antonio Negri, eds, *Crisi e organizzazione operaia*. Milano: Feltrinelli.

1976. *Proletari e stato: Per una discussione su autonomia operaia e compromesso storico*. Milano: Feltrinelli.

1977. *La forma stato: Per la critica dell'economia polilica della Costituzione*. Milano: Feltrinelli.

1978. *Il dominio e il sabotaggio: Sul metodo marxista della trasformazione sociale*. Milano: Feltrinelli.

2003. *Time for Revolution*. New York: Continuum.

O'Donnell, Mike and Sue Sharpe. 2000. *Uncertain Masculinities: Youth, Ethnicity and Class in Contemporary Britain*. London: Routledge.

Olavarría, José. 2001. *Y todos querían ser (buenos) padres: Varones de Santiago de Chile en conflicto*. Santiago: FLACSO-Chile.

Organization for Economic Cooperation and Development (OECD). 2005. *Teachers Matter: Attracting, Developing and Retaining Effective Teachers*. Paris: OECD Publishing.

Orloff, Ann Shola. 2002. 'Explaining US welfare reform: power, gender, race and the US policy legacy', *Critical Social Policy* 22(1): 96–118.

Palme, Olof. 1972. 'The Emancipation of Man', *Journal of Social Issues* 28(2): 237–46.

Patel, Sujata, ed. 2010. *ISA Handbook of Diverse Sociological Traditions*. London: Sage.

Paz, Octavio. [1950]1990. *The Labyrinth of Solitude*. Enlarged edn. London: Penguin.

Pease, Bob. 1997. *Men and Sexual Politics: Towards a Profeminist Practice*. Adelaide: Dulwich Centre.

Peters, Michael. 1995. *Education and the Postmodern Condition*. Westport, CT: Bergin and Garvey.

Plaatje, Solomon. T. [1916] 1982. *Native Life in South Africa: Before and Since the European War and the Boer Rebellion*. New edn. Braamfontein: Ravan Press.

Pocock, Barbara. 2003. *The Work/Life Collision: What Work is Doing to Australians and What to Do About It*. Sydney: Federation Press.

Power, Michael. 1997. *The Audit Society: Rituals of Verification*. Oxford: Oxford University Press.

Ptacek, James. 1988. 'Why do men batter their wives?', pp. 133–57 in Kersti Yllö and Michele Bograd, eds, *Feminist Perspectives on Wife Abuse*. Newbury Park, CA: Sage Publications.

Ranson, Stewart, Jane Martin, Penny McKeown and Margaret Arnott. 2003. 'Parents as volunteer citizens: voice, deliberation and governance', *Parliamentary Affairs* 56: 716–32.

Reay, Diane. 2001. 'Finding or losing yourself? Working-class relationships to education', *Journal of Education Policy* 16: 333–46.

Reay, Diane and Stephen J. Ball. 1997. '"Spoilt for choice": The working classes and educational markets', *Oxford Review of Education* 23 (1): 89–101.

Red Notes. 1979. *Working Class Autonomy and the Crisis: Italian Marxist Texts of the Theory and Practice of a Class Movement: 1964–79.* London: Red Notes and CSE Books.

Reid, Alan. 2003. 'Understanding teachers' work: is there still a place for labour process theory?' *British Journal of Sociology of Education* 24(5): 559–73.

Richter, Linda and Robert Morrell, eds. 2006. *Baba: Men and Fatherhood in South Africa.* Cape Town: HSRC Press.

Rigi, Jakob. 2003. 'The conditions of post-Soviet dispossessed youth and work in Almaty, Kazakhstan', *Critique of Anthropology* 23(1): 35–49.

Risman, Barbara J. 1986. 'Can men "mother"? Life as a single father', *Family Relations* 35: 95–102.

Robinson, Jennifer. 2006. *Ordinary Cities: Between Modernity and Development.* London: Routledge.

Roy, Rahul. 2003. '*Exploring Masculinities – A Travelling Seminar.' Agenda* and abstracts. Unpublished manuscript supplied to author.

Sammons, Pam, Christopher Day, Alison Kington, Gu Qing, Gordon Stobart and Rebecca Smees. 2007. 'Exploring variations in teachers' work, lives and their effects on pupils: key findings and implications from a longitudinal mixed-method study', *British Educational Research Journal* 33(5): 681–701.

Scheler, Max. [1924] 1992. *On Feeling, Knowing and Valuing: Selected Writings.* Edited by Harold J. Bershady. Chicago: Chicago University Press.

Schofield, Toni. 2004. *Boutique Health? Gender and Equity in Health Policy.* Sydney: Australian Health Policy Institute.

Schofield, Toni and Susan Goodwin. 2005. 'Advancing gender reform in large-scale organisations: a new approach for practitioners and researchers', *Policy and Society* 24(4): 25–44.

Sciascia, Leonardo. 1978. *L'affaire Moro*, 2nd edn. Palermo: Sellerio. [Translation: *The Moro Affair and the Mystery of Majorana*, New York: New York Review Books, 2004.]

Segal, Lynne. 1997. *Slow Motion: Changing Masculinities, Changing Men.* 2nd edn. London: Virago.

Sen, Amartya. 1999. *Development as Freedom*. Oxford: Oxford University Press.

Serequeberhan, Tsenay, ed. 1991. *African Philosophy: The Essential Readings*. New York: Paragon House.

Shariati, Ali. 1986. *What Is to be Done? The Enlightened Thinkers and an Islamic Renaissance*. Ed. Farhang Rajaee. Houston: Institute for Research and Islamic Studies.

Sharp, Geoff. 1983. 'Intellectuals in transition', *Arena* 65: 84–95.

Silber, Irina Carlota. 2004. 'Mothers/fighters/citizens: Violence and disillusionment in post-war El Salvador'. *Gender and History*, 16 (3): 561–87.

Smart, Barry. 2003. *Economy, Culture and Society: A Sociological Critique of Neo-Liberalism*. Buckingham: Open University Press.

Smith, Dorothy. 1990. *The Conceptual Practices of Power: A Feminist Sociology of Knowledge*. London: Routledge.

Sommers, Christina Hoff. 2000. *The War against Boys: How Misguided Feminism is Harming Our Young Men*. New York: Simon and Schuster.

Song, Jesook. 2006. 'Family breakdown and invisible homeless women: Neoliberal governance during the Asian debt crisis in South Korea, 1997–2001'. *Positions*, 14 (1): 37–66.

Stacey, Judith. 2011. *Unhitched: Love, Marriage, and Family Values from West Hollywood to Western China*. New York, New York University Press.

Steinmetz, George, ed. 2011. *Sociology and Empire: Colonial Studies and the Imperial Entanglements of a Discipline*. Durham: Duke University Press.

Stevenson, Howard. 2007. 'Restructuring teachers: work and trade unions in England: bargaining for change?' *American Educational Research Journal* 44(2): 224–51.

Sun Yat-sen. [1927]1975. *San Min Chu I: The Three Principles of the People*. New York, Da Capo Press.

Taga Futoshi. 2001. *Dansei no Jenda Keisei: 'Otoko-Rashisa' no Yuragi no Naka de*. Tokyo: Toyokan Shuppan-sha.

——— 2007. 'The trends of discourse on fatherhood and father's conflict in Japan'. Paper to 15th Biennial Conference of Japanese Studies Association of Australia, Canberra.

Teese, Richard and J. Polesel. 2003. *Undemocratic Schooling*. Melbourne: Melbourne University Press.

Tempels, Placide. [1945]1959. *Bantu Philosophy*. Paris: Présence Africaine.

Tinsman, Heidi. 2000. 'Reviving feminist materialism: gender and neoliberalism in Pinochet's Chile', *Signs* 26(1): 145–88.

Tronti, Mario. [1966] 1971. *Operai e capital*. 2nd edn. Torino: Einaudi.

United Nations. [1979] 1989. *Convention on the Elimination of All Forms of Discrimination Against Women*. New York: Department of Public Information, United Nations.

United Nations. [1995 and 2000] 2001. *Beijing Declaration and Platform for Action, with the Beijing +5 Political Declaration and Outcome Document*. New York: Department of Public Information, United Nations.

United Nations Commission on the Status of Women. 2004. *The Role of Men and Boys in Achieving Gender Equality: Agreed Conclusions*. Available online at http://www.un.org/womenwatch/daw/csw48/ac-men-auv.pdf

United Nations Development Programme. 2003. *Human Development Report 2003*. New York: UNDP and Oxford University Press.

Vahdat, Farzin. 2002. *God and Juggernaut: Iran's Intellectual Encounter with Modernity*. Syracuse, NY: Syracuse, University Press.

Valdés, Teresa and José Olavarría. 1998. 'Ser hombre en Santiago de Chile: A pesar de todo, un mismo modelo'. pp. 12–36 in Teresa Valdés and José Olavarría, eds, *Masculinidades y equidad de género en América Latina*. Santiago: FLACSO/UNFPA.

Vavrus, Mary Douglas. 2007. 'Opting out moms in the news: selling new traditionalism in the new millenium', *Feminist Media Studies* 7 (1), 47–63.

Victorian Institute of Teaching. 2008. Standards for graduating teachers. Accessed 2009 at http://www.vit.vic.edu.au/content.asp?DocumentID=5

Viveros Vigoya, Mara. 2001. 'Contemporary Latin American perspectives on masculinity', *Men and Masculinities* 3(3): 237–60.

Wajcman, Judy. 1999. *Managing Like a Man: Women and Men in Corporate Management*. Cambridge: Polity.

2004. *TechnoFeminism*. Cambridge: Polity.

Wall, Glenda. 2001. 'Moral constructions of motherhood in breastfeeding discourse', *Gender and Society* 15(4): 592–610.

Weber, Everard. 2007. 'Globalization, "glocal" development and teachers' work: a research agenda', *Review of Educational Research* 77(3): 279–309.

Weigt, Jill. 2006. 'Compromises to care work: the social organization of mothers' experiences in the low-wage labor market after welfare reform', *Social Problems* 53(3): 332–51.

Wetherell, Margaret and Nigel Edley. 1999. 'Negotiating hegemonic masculinity: imaginary positions and psycho-discursive practices', *Feminism and Psychology* 9(3): 335–56.

White, Sara C. 2000. 'Did the earth move? the hazards of bringing men and masculinities into gender and development', *IDS Bulletin* 31(2): 33–41.

Widersprüche. 1998. 'Multioptionale Männlichkeiten?' no. 67, whole issue.

Wiredu, Kwasi. 1980. *Philosophy and an African Culture*. Cambridge: Cambridge University Press.

Wisselgren, Per. 2000. *Samhällets kartläggare: Lorénska stiftelsen, den sociala frågan och samhällsvetenskapens formering i Sverige 1830–1920*. Diss. Stockholm/Stehag: Symposion.

Yeatman, Anna. 1990. *Bureaucrats, Technocrats, Femocrats: Essays on the Contemporary Australian State*. Sydney: Allen and Unwin.

Index

Aboriginal communities and cultures, Australia 71, 122, 162, *see also* land rights
Afghanistan 137, 159
Africa 42, 108, 121
African National Congress 150
African philosophy 112, 122, 126–7, 132
AIDS *see* HIV/AIDS
Akiwowo, Akinsola 115, 133
al-Afghani, Sayyid Jamal ad-Din 111–12, 114–15
Al-e Ahmad, 113, 114
Amin, Samir 43, 127
Arena (Australian journal), thesis on intellectuals 91, 92, 97
Australia 11, 43, 51, 54, 92, 109–10, 131–3, 157
    left 4, 159
    school education in 59, 63, 71, 74, 78
Australian Business Council 74, 81
automation 31, 109

Bakare-Yusuf, Bibi 115
Balandier, Georges 110
Bauman, Zygmunt 91, 92
Beck, Ulrich 138
Becker, Gary 49
Beijing Declaration and Platform for Action 12
Benda, Lucien 91
Benin 120
Bjerrum Nielsen, Harriet 48, 49
Bly, Robert 8
Bolivia 51, 164
Brazil 23, 50, 106
Britain 16, 49, 75, 77
Bukharin, Nikolai 107
Bulbeck, Chilla 117, 118
Burawoy, Michael 6, 108, 116, 118

Canada 14, 53, 119
capitalism 139, 145, 152, 157, 160, *see also* corporations
Cardoso, Fernando Henrique 113
Catholic Church 20, 59, 70

CEPAL (Comision Economica para America Latina) 114, 155
children, care of 12, 14, 30
  as breadwinners 50
Chile 16, 43, 47
China 110, 114, 157, 160–1
class, social 14, 58, 83, 142
  creative 2, 159
  middle 29, 58
  ruling 10, 52, 59, 88, 148, 161
  working 58, 65, 88, 142, 146, 148, 153, autonomy 143, 151, 153, communities 65, 88, families 58–72, 72, education 62, 75, 155, youth 60
climate change 1, 2, 4, 161
CODESRIA (Council for the Development of Social Science Research in Africa 117, 130
colonialism 6, 41, 110, 116, 133, see also neocolonialism
commodification 55–6
communism 141–2, 148–9, 154
computer technology 38, 78, 86, 94–6
Comte, Auguste 90, 104–6
Comtean sociology 116, 118
Connell, Raewyn 104, 110, 147
corporations (business) 26, 42, 80, 98, 114, 150
Costa Rica 47
culture 10, 15, 27
  optimism and pessimism in 100
curriculum, school 76, 78, 84, 86

decolonization 108, 123
Deleuze, Gilles 140
democracy 104, 156
Deutscher, Max 6
Disadvantaged Schools Programme 156
Donner, Henrike 53
Duménil, Gérard 42

Ecuador 164
education 12, 39, 44, 52, 60, 76, 81, see also teachers, technical and further education
  multicultural 58
  subject choice in 65, 68
Eire 45
El Salvador 54
environment 2, 22, 156, 163, see also climate change
epistemology 109, 114–16
Equal Employment Opportunity (EEO) 14, 22, 37, 44
ethnicity 19, 83
ethnophilosophy 125, 124, 126

Faletto, Enzo 113
family 9, 41, 44, 58–72
  relationships 43, 44, 49
Fanon, Frantz 115, 124
fathers and fatherhood 9, 11, 16, 45, 57
  'new' 8, 52
feminism 8, 25, 33, 116, 159
  Women's Liberation Movement 116, 155–6, 165
Free University (Sydney) 155

Gandhi, Mohandas Karamchand 112
Garretón, Manuel 113
Gay Liberation Movement 19, 155
gender 10, 11, 18, 25, 36, 44, 55, 83, 117
  change 18, 25, 26
  division of labour in households 18, 37, 38
  equality 3– 4, 7–15, 18–22, 25–7, 35–9, 44, 75
  inequality 13, 21, 33, 36–7
  neutrality 35–8, 39
  regimes 25–40, 52, 70
  research and theory 115–17
gender-based violence 2, 12, 14–16
Germany 8, 15

Ghana 123
Giddens, Anthony 109, 138
'glass ceiling' 2, 36, 37
global
    metropole 42–3, 53, 92, 99,
        101–112, 115–118, 127, 133–4,
        150
    periphery 105–114, 118, 120–135
globalization 10, 90, 101, 109,
    117, 146, 150, *see also* quasi-
    globalization
Gouldner, Alvin 91
Grace, Gerald 81

Han, Clara 50
Hartcher, Peter (journalist) 161
Hau'ofa, Epeli 114
HIV/AIDS 2, 6, 11, 19, 117, 162–3
Hoadley, Ursula 85
Holter, Øystein Gullvag 8, 15, 17, 45,
    48
Hopenhayn, Martín 86
Hountondji, Paulin J. 4, 19, 106, 115,
    119–135

imperialism 107, 111, 112, *see also*
    colonialism
India 14, 112, 114
Indonesia 9
industrialization 41, 104
intellectual work and workers 74,
    89–102
intellectuals 90, 92, 154, *see also*
    teachers, ulama
International Monetary Fund (IMF)
    42, 157.
Internet use 95, 158
Iran 92, 113
Iraq 137, 159
Islam 89, 99, 100, 111, 134

Japan 9, 15, 45, 53, 106
Jolly, Margaret 110

Kagamé, Alexis 123
Kartini, Raden Adjeng 111
Kazakhstan 51
Kenyatta, Jomo 112
Keynesian policies 42, 145, 155
Khan, Said Ahmad 14
Korea 43
Kosik, Karel 4

Labor Party, Australian 71, 154, 157–8
land rights, indigenous 112, 155, 162
Latin America 42, 43, 46, 86, 112,
    157
Lévy, Dominique 42
'long hours' culture 51
Lukács, Gyorgy 119, 120

managers 30, 77, 100
Mannheim, Karl 91, 107, 119, 120
Mannon, Susan 47
market ideology *see* neoliberalism
Marx, Karl 104, 107, 144, 160
Marxism 111, 139, 142, 148, 159
masculinities 7–24, 45–6, 55
men and boys 7–24, *see also*
    masculinities
    capacity for change 16–19
    in gender equality politics 10–12,
        16–21
    interests 12–16, 33
Messner, Michael 21, 53
metropole *see* global metropole
Mexico 9, 113, 160
Mill, John Stuart 14, 18
Moghadam, Valentine M. 117
Mohanty, Chandra Talpade 117
Morrell, Robert 10, 18
mothers and motherhood 47–8, 53,
    56–7

Nandy, Ashis 112
Negri, Antonio 4, 136–53, 161
négritude 112, 121, 124–5

neocolonialism 110, 160
neoliberalism 2, 4, 19, 25, 37–9, 42,
46–7, 52, 54, 59–60, 71–2, 85,
98–102, 113, 152, 156–9, 162,
164, *see also* privatization
and teaching 77, 80, 83
depresión neoliberal 54–5
in organizations 44, 82, *see also*
managers
project 20, 49, 55–7, 69, 79, 85
regimes 41, 52, 53, 163
Netherlands 111
new left 121, 142, 155–7, 164
New Zealand 43, 157
Nicaragua 47, 54

occupations 18, 85, 97
ontoformativity (of social practice) 4,
5, 87
ontology 122, 123
Organization for Economic
Cooperation and Development
(OECD) 74, 87, 118
Overland (magazine) 154, 159, 165,
166

Pacific islands and islanders 42, 70–1,
110, 114
parent/child relationships 3, 43–4,
63–5
parenthood 17, 41–57, 66, *see also*
fatherhood, motherhood
Parsons, Talcott 108, 109, 116
patriarchy 9, 55, 117, *see also* gender
inequality
Paz, Octavio 113
Plaatje, Solomon 112
Pocock, Barbara 46, 54
postcolonial societies 110, 114, 116,
159
power 27, 100, 111
Pram Factory (theatre) 155
Prebisch, Raul 113, 115

private sector 20, 138
schools 42, 52, 59, 72
privatization (of public assets) 26, 47,
50, 157
public sector 20, 26, 28, 38–9, 42, 46
cuts 47, *see also* neoliberalism
schools 20, 52, 56, 58, 60, 69, 72,
155
public service 40, 42

quasi-globalization 99, 101
queer politics 158, 165

race and racism 6, 14, 160
red brigades (Italy) 142, 148
religion 15, 19, 83, 110
research and research methods (social
science) 3, 5, 106, 108–9
Rigi, Jakob 51, 54
Robinson, Jennifer 118
Roy, Rahul 9, 18
ruling class *see* class, social
Rwanda 123

'salaryman' model of husband/
fatherhood 45
Santiago de Chile 50, 155
Saudi Arabia 161
Scandinavia 8, 16
Sciascia, Leonardo 143
science 3, 119, *see also* sociology,
research and research methods
self-valorization (autovalorizzazione)
147, 148, 153
sexism 16, 20, 28, 31, 33, 39, 45
sexuality 10, 19, 110
Shariati, Ali 18, 92, 115
Singapore 161
Smith, Dorothy 119
socialism 155, 164
sociology 2
history of 103–18
of knowledge 119–20, 135

Somalia 160
Song, Jesook 43
South Africa 10, 18, 50, 76, 85
Soviet Union 43, 51
Sri Lanka 160
Stacey, Judith 2
state, 25–6, *see also* public sector
Sun, Yat-sen 110–11, 115

Taga Futoshi 45, 46
teachers 73–88
technical and vocational education
    60–1, 63, 69, 71–2, 76, 85
Tempels, Placide 122, 125
terrorism 89, 148
Tinsman, Heidi 47
Tronti, Mario 142

ulama (Muslim scholars) 111
United Nations,
    Commission on the Status of
        Women (CSW) 22
    Convention on the Elimination
        of all forms of Discrimination
        Against Women (CEDAW) 10
    General Assembly, 23rd Special
        Session (2000) 12
unions (of workers) 20, 42, 46, 71, 97,
    154–8
United States 15, 19

universities and colleges 27, 43, 59–60,
    75, 98

Vaerting, Mathilde 107, 116
Valdés, Teresa 12, 16
Vavrus, Mary 48
Venezuela 164
Vietnam 160
Vigoya, Mara Viveros 46
violence 8, 9, 22–3, *see also* gender-
    based violence, war
vocational education *see* technical and
    vocational education

war 18, 41, 137
Weber, Everard 76, 85
welfare state 20, 39, 157, *see also*
    Keynesian policies
Wiredu, Kwasi 125, 126
women 23, 32, 37, 47, 88, 160
Women's Liberation Movement 116,
    155, 156, 165
work/life balance 18, 27, 35, 43–4,
    46, 54
working class *see* class, social

Yeatman, Anna 26

Zaire 125
Zapatistas 139, 150